PENGUIN  CLASSICS

THE BERNARD SHAW LIBRARY

CANDIDA

GEORGE BERNARD SHAW was born in Dublin in 1856. Although essentially shy, he created in his journalism the persona of G.B.S., the showman, satirist, controversialist, critic, pundit, wit, intellectual buffoon, and dramatist. Commentators brought a new adjective into English: *Shavian*, a term used to embody all his brilliant qualities.

After his arrival in London in 1876, he became an active Socialist and a brilliant platform speaker. He wrote on many social and political issues of the day, from war to the "Irish question" to Socialism. When he undertook his own education at the British Museum Reading Room, he developed a keen interest in cultural subjects, leading to a prolific output of music, art, and theater reviews, as well as five novels and some short fiction.

Shaw remains best known as a dramatist and was closely associated with the intellectual revival of British theater in the late nineteenth and early twentieth centuries. His many plays (the full canon runs to fifty-two) include *Widowers' Houses, The Philanderer, Mrs. Warren's Profession, Arms and the Man, Candida, The Man of Destiny, You Never Can Tell, The Devil's Disciple, Caesar and Cleopatra, Captain Brassbound's Conversion, Man and Superman, John Bull's Other Island, Major Barbara, The Doctor's Dilemma, Misalliance, Androcles and the Lion, Pygmalion, Heartbreak House, Back to Methuselah, Saint Joan, The Apple Cart, Too True to Be Good,* and *The Millionairess.*

In 1925, Shaw was awarded the Nobel Prize in Literature. In 1939, he won an Academy Award for the screenplay for the 1938 film *Pygmalion,* and he is still the only Nobel laureate to win the Oscar. He died in 1950.

PETER GAHAN, a writer and graduate of Trinity College, Dublin, has written several articles and reviews on Bernard Shaw. His book *Shaw Shadows: Rereading the Texts of Bernard Shaw* was published in 2004 by the University Press of Florida, and he serves on the editorial board of *SHAW: The Annual of Bernard Shaw Studies,* published by Pennsylvania State University Press. He lives in Los Angeles and works in the film industry.

DAN H. LAURENCE, series editor for the works of Shaw in Penguin, was literary adviser to the Shaw Estate until his retirement in 1990. He edited Shaw's *Collected Letters,* his *Collected Plays with their Prefaces, Shaw's Music,* and (with Daniel Leary) *The Complete Prefaces.*

BERNARD SHAW

Candida

A PLEASANT PLAY

Introduction by
PETER GAHAN

Definitive text under the editorial supervision of
DAN H. LAURENCE

PENGUIN BOOKS

PENGUIN BOOKS

Published by Penguin Group

Penguin Group (USA) Inc., 375 Hudson Street, New York, New York 10014, U.S.A.
Penguin Group (Canada), 90 Eglinton Avenue East, Suite 700, Toronto, Ontario, Canada M4P 2Y3
(a division of Pearson Penguin Canada Inc.)
Penguin Books Ltd, 80 Strand, London WC2R 0RL, England
Penguin Ireland, 25 St Stephen's Green, Dublin 2, Ireland (a division of Penguin Books Ltd)
Penguin Group (Australia), 250 Camberwell Road, Camberwell, Victoria 3124, Australia
(a division of Pearson Australia Group Pty Ltd)
Penguin Books India Pvt Ltd, 11 Community Centre, Panchsheel Park, New Delhi – 110 017, India
Penguin Group (NZ), cnr Airborne and Rosedale Roads, Albany, Auckland 1310, New Zealand
(a division of Pearson New Zealand Ltd)
Penguin Books (South Africa) (Pty) Ltd, 24 Sturdee Avenue, Rosebank, Johannesburg 2196, South Africa

Penguin Books Ltd, Registered Offices:
80 Strand, London WC2R 0RL, England

This edition with an introduction by Peter Gahan first published in Penguin Books 2006

Applications for permission to give stock and amateur performances of Bernard Shaw's plays in the United
States of America and Canada should be made to Samuel French, Inc., 45 West 25th Street, New York,
New York 10010. In all other cases, whether for stage, radio, or television, applications should be made
to The Society of Authors, 84 Drayton Gardens, London SW10 9SD, England.

LIBRARY OF CONGRESS CATALOGING IN PUBLICATION DATA
Shaw, Bernard, 1856–1950.
Candida : a pleasant play / Bernard Shaw ; definitive text under the editorial supervision
of Dan H. Laurence ; introduction by Peter Gahan.
p.   cm.—(Penguin Classics)
ISBN 0 14 30.3978 4
1. Laurence, Dan H.   II. Title.   III. Series.
PR5363.C3 2006
822'.912—dc22   2005056725

Set in Sabon

Contents

Introduction

In the first half of 1894, Bernard Shaw saw a good deal of fellow Irish writer and poet William Butler Yeats. Yeats's short play *The Land of Heart's Desire* was the curtain raiser for Shaw's fourth play, *Arms and the Man*, in a season of plays by Irish writers at the Avenue Theatre, London, produced by actress Florence Farr with financial backing from Annie Horniman, that would prove a precursor of the future Irish Literary Theatre at the Abbey Theatre in Dublin.[1] Yeats, Farr, and Horniman were all involved in an occult group called the Order of the Golden Dawn, which reached back to the mystery festivals of the ancient world for inspiration. In his autobiography, Yeats described Florence Farr, Shaw's mistress and Yeats's would-be lover, as possessing "a tranquil beauty like that of Demeter's image near the British Museum reading room door."[2]

Shaw must have been familiar with this fourth-century B.C. Demeter statue of Knidos, as on most days of his early working life in London, the Socialist revolutionary, art and music critic, author of *The Quintessence of Ibsenism* (1891), and aspiring dramatist would pass through the door of the famous Reading Room, where he spent hours reading, writing, and conversing with scholars. An autodidact like Yeats, he later described the place as one of the constituent colleges of the university he never attended. Shaw absorbed an enormous amount of information in that library, and a great deal of it—including Demeter—worked its way into the detail of *Candida: A Mystery*, written later in 1894, and his other plays.

Candida probably deserves to be called Shaw's masterpiece, if we take that word to mean the particular work a craftsman creates after years as apprentice and journeyman to prove a mastery in his chosen art. With *Candida*, the thirty-eight-year-old writer evidenced a new certainty in his capabilities within a medium he had come to relatively late in life; his first play, *Widowers' Houses*, had been completed only two years earlier. After finishing the first draft of *Candida* (the holograph manuscript gives December 7, 1894), Shaw wrote fellow playwright Henry Arthur Jones on December 24:

> Like you, I write plays because I like it, and because I cannot remember any period in my life when I could help inventing people and scenes. I am not a storyteller: things occur to me as scenes, with action and dialogue—as moments, developing themselves out of their own vitality . . . a drama of pure feeling, wittily expressed . . . you will at once detect an enormous assumption on my part that I am a man of genius. But what can I do—on what other assumption am I to proceed if I am to write plays at all? You will detect the further assumption that the public . . . will (twenty years hence) see feeling and reality where now they see nothing but mere intellectual sword play and satire.[3]

Shaw did not have to wait twenty years; he waited only ten. When *Candida* was produced at the Royal Court Theatre in London for a series of matinee performances in 1904, with Harley Granville Barker as the poet in love with both beauty and the eponymous Candida, Shaw's career as a dramatist—a patchy one at best up to that point (even the London *Arms and the Man* production, successful for Shaw personally, had been a commercial failure)—was jump-started, and this association with Granville Barker at the Royal Court inaugurated what we now call twentieth-century British theater.

Candida is Shaw's simplest play to produce in terms of its single setting and six characters: the Rev. James Mavor Morell; his wife, Candida; his father-in-law, Burgess; his assistant Lexy Mill; his secretary Prossy (short for Proserpine) Garnett; and the stranger whom he brings into his home, the young poet Eugene Marchbanks. Simple also is the surface action of this "pleasant play" as a domestic drama of Ibsenist realism. In

Candida the radical Socialist clergyman, living and working with his family in a lower-middle-class area of northeast London (the sociopolitical background to the play is described at length in Shaw's opening stage directions), has discovered the penniless homeless poet (albeit an earl's nephew from a comfortable background) and has brought him to live in his home, which is dominated by his beautiful and fascinating wife, Candida, daughter of the rather coarse self-made factory owner, the aptly named Burgess.[4] A parody of the art of courtly love, in which the poet falls in love with the clergyman's wife, and a parody of Ibsen's *A Doll's House*, in which the husband—not the wife—is shown as the doll, Shaw's play ends with neither wife nor husband walking out of the house, but the poet. In coming to understand the imaginative illusion that is his infatuation with Candida, Eugene discovers his poetic vocation to be more important than domesticity, while the Morell marriage remains intact, though shaken.

But Shaw's writing, like the music of his artistic hero Mozart, is never as simple as it seems. So perhaps we should read this play contrariwise as a prime example of the complexity of Shaw's dramaturgy. *Candida* invokes drama's origins in the ancient world, while seeking to encompass Wagner's notion of *Gesamtkunstwerk* ("total work of art") in its re-creation of Greek tragedy, to include the whole experience of what we call theater. But even this grandiose ambition is not as simple as it seems.

Shaw, who insisted that "classical literature is made up nine-tenths of allusion," gleefully boasted of the authors whom he pillaged.[5] In the final scene Candida declares to the two men bidding for her affection, "I am up for auction, it seems." Shaw probably borrowed this auction idea from Henry Arthur Jones's play *The Masqueraders,* which had opened earlier that year in London.[6] And the young poet's bid for her that ends with "My heart's need" probably alludes to the title of Yeats's short play, mentioned above; some critics have even considered Yeats to be the model for Marchbanks.

More important, *Candida* hearkens back to classical tragedy. The Dionysia, the annual drama festival of fifth-century B.C.

Athens, was held in honor of Dionysus (or Bacchus), the young, headstrong god of wine and, like the corn goddess Demeter, a benefactor of mankind. As Nietzsche explained in his *Birth of Tragedy* (1872), all the tragic heroes are masks of the god, where the god indeed is the ultimate spectator of his own drama.[7] We should not, therefore, pass lightly over stage directions in *Candida* (ostensibly a comedy) that invoke tragedy, such as "Frightened at the tragic mask presented to her" or "like a man witnessing a tragedy." Dionysus was the harbinger of a new religion among the ancient Greeks, and Shaw, who himself wanted to bring about a revival of religious feeling, inscribes into his text the madness associated with the followers of Dionysus. As a running joke, almost every character is called "mad" at one time or another during the play. Especially "mad" is the boy-man god figure, the poet Marchbanks, who in Dionysian fashion "dances about excitedly" while "snapping his fingers wildly" in act III. Yet another nod to the god of the vine comes in what Shaw sarcastically describes in the preface as "the drunken scene . . . which has been much appreciated, I am told, in Aberdeen." This scene, also in act III, occurs when three of the characters return from Morell's lecture drunk, both from Morell's oratory and from having taken champagne—an association set up in act I when the poet accuses the preacher of exciting his listeners "until they behaved exactly as if they were drunk." The Dionysia were held in the month of Elaphebolion, which we now call March, and this is possibly alluded to in the poet's name, as names are seldom accidental in Shaw's plays. When Shaw later described Marchbanks leaving the Morell home at the end as "like a god going back to his heaven," the god he had in mind was probably Dionysus, although he would also have been thinking of his Christian equivalent, Christ—both gods died and were reborn.[8]

Despite the connections between Shaw and Yeats, *Candida* is not a Yeatsean occult text awaiting divination. It shows, rather, affinities with the writing of another, younger Irish contemporary, James Joyce. Indeed there is evidence that Joyce, suffering from a certain amount of "anxiety of influence," sought to obscure Shaw's influence both on his vocation as writer—as Promethean artist

in exile—and on his writing technique, which resulted in a literary realism dense with allusion but also playful in terms of
genre and form.[9] We might even ponder *Candida*'s similarity to
the situation in later parts of *Ulysses* in which Bloom brings the
young homeless writer Stephen Dedalus (a name that com-
bines, as Shaw's play does, the Christian and Greek worlds)
into a home dominated by an earth goddess–like wife, Molly (a
synonym of Mary, and Shaw famously referred to Candida as
"the Virgin Mother and nobody else").[10] *Candida*, which
reaches back to the origins of European drama, reaches forward also to the coming twentieth century, to the young writers in Joyce's *Portrait of the Artist as a Young Man* and Eugene
O'Neill's *Ah, Wilderness!* (in which the young Marchbanks-
like protagonist reads *Candida*), as well as to Robert Graves's
theory of poetry in *The White Goddess* (Demeter in one incar-
nation).

On October 2, 1894, according to the holograph manuscript, Shaw began composition of *Candida: A Domestic Play
in Three Acts*. The first edition of the play, published in 1898 in
the second volume—"containing the four Pleasant Plays"—of
the groundbreaking *Plays Pleasant and Unpleasant*, begins "A
fine October morning . . . ." Later editions, including this one,
return the text to its time of writing: "A fine morning in October 1894 . . . ." Earlier that year, Shaw had made two trips to
continental Europe. As a music critic, he traveled to Germany
in July to attend the Bayreuth Festival (where Richard Wagner
hoped to revive the religious spirit of Greek tragedy), twice seeing Wagner's last opera, *Parsifal*, which at the time was per-
formed only at Bayreuth. This religious, ritualistic music-drama
for initiates would leave its traces on the text of *Candida*: on
Marchbanks as a Parsifalian "pure fool" (*der reine Tor*), who
brings salvation through compassionate knowing (*durch
Mitleid wissend*) to the wasteland Christian civilization had
become; on Candida as a Kundry figure bifurcated between
sexual temptress and maternal healer; on its ritual gestures;
and on its religious medievalism (which Shaw associated with
the art of the Pre-Raphaelites, their love of Arthurian legend,
Chaucer, and the literature of courtly love).[11] Two weeks after

he began writing *Candida*, Shaw delivered a lecture on *Parsifal*
to the Guild of St. Matthew organized by his friend Stewart
Headlam, the Christian Socialist clergyman. In the first scene of
the play the Christian Socialist clergyman Morell reads an article by Headlam and news about the Guild of St. Matthew in
The Church Reformer, and the lecture Morell gives to the guild
between acts II and III becomes pivotal to the action.[12] With
the music-drama *Parsifal*, Wagner aimed to create a
Gesamtkunstwerk that, with Greek tragedy as a model, would
combine several distinct arts, use a mythological background,
have a religious purpose, depict human-divine relations, and
provide a communal social experience. As an antidote to the
well-made plays and the police court dramas that comprised so
much of late nineteenth-century London theater, Shaw, in in-
voking both the classical world and Wagner's operatic reforms,
aimed to produce with his Ibsenist domestic drama *Candida*
what can best be described as a *textual Gesamtkunstwerk*.

Candida can be seen to fulfill all five of Wagner's goals described above. It incorporates several different art forms, working into its text music (both the narrative themes and the
leitmotif or leading motifs technique of *Parsifal*), painting (particularly that of the Pre-Raphaelites and Titian), literature (art
of courtly love, poetry, and Chaucer), and drama (Greek tragedy,
medieval mystery plays, and Ibsen). It employs mythology, referring to both Greek (Demeter and Persephone, and Dionysus)
and Christian (Virgin Mary and her Son) myths. It proposes a
revival of religion; as the preface explains, "Religion was alive
again, coming back upon men, even upon clergymen, with such
power that not the Church of England itself could keep it out."
It describes a period of transition in the human-divine relation
(as with Dionysus for the Greeks, or Christianity for the Romans, or the Renaissance for the Middle Ages) in a modern re-
action against the age of rationalism and materialism. And,
finally, by weaving Socialism, moral preaching, and poetry into
a dramatic situation, the play in the theater seeks to become a
socially regenerative communal experience—a surprising ambition, perhaps, for what appears to be an intimate domestic
drama.

Shaw writes in the preface: "In the Autumn of 1894 I spent a few weeks in Florence, where I occupied myself with the religious art of the Middle Ages and its destruction by the Renascence. . . . The time was ripe for a modern pre-Raphaelite play." On this art study tour of Italy, Shaw displayed an interest in figurative representations of the Virgin Mother that would also leave its mark on his fifth play, begun shortly after returning to London. On his journey to Bayreuth earlier that year, he had gone out of his way to see a Holbein Madonna in Darmstadt. In Italy, he saw Madonnas by Botticelli, Correggio, and others. For a play boasting its Pre-Raphaelitism, however, Shaw ironically chose, according to the handwritten manuscript, a "large photograph of the [Raphael] Madonna di San Sisto" to adorn the wall above the mantelpice over the fire, before settling in the printed version on "a large autotype of the chief figure in Titian's Assumption of the Virgin." Shaw wanted with this text to dramatize a revival of religion, associated with the art of the Pre-Raphaelites in his own time, that would signal a historical transition between an old and new religion. But he also needed to suggest what would result from this transition; hence he needed to balance the Pre-Raphaelite atmosphere of the play with Titian's painting, a gift from Marchbanks. This transition, according to the preface, is represented in the play by the conflict between preacher and poet: "To distil the quintessential drama from Pre-Raphaelitism, medieval or modern, it must be shewn at its best in conflict with the first broken, nervous, stumbling attempts to formulate its own revolt against itself as it develops into something higher." There is knowing irony too in the disjunction between the play's immature poet and the confidence of Titian's painting, representative of what he might achieve.

One other reason Shaw might have preferred Titian's *Assumption* to Raphael's *Sistine Madonna* to adorn the set for *Candida*, to which he gave the subtitle *A Mystery*, is because it depicts the fourth Glorious Mystery of the Rosary. Cults of the Blessed Virgin flourished in the Middle Ages, and the prayer practice of the rosary (repeatedly saying ten Hail Marys for every one Our Father), reputedly devised by St. Dominic, involves contemplation of the Sorrowful, Joyful, and Glorious Mysteries of the lives of the Virgin Mary and her Son. The Morell parsonage, we may note, is called St. Dominic's. Further, marriage is understood in most Christian denominations as a mystery expressing the relation between Christ and the church or the people. In act I, Morell discourses pompously to Eugene on the virtues of Christian marriage, and the text plumbs to its depths the mystery of the Morell marriage, whose drama in the surface action is counterpointed to that mystical marriage of initiation between Candida and Eugene.

But *mystery* has other connotations in the context of this play. Shaw explained in a letter of August 18, 1906, to his German translator Siegfried Trebitsch: "I often have to go behind the popular use of a word into its etymology to get it quite right."[13] In this respect, his use of the word *mystery* reveals the many-sidedness, the multiplicity of meaning, and the (inter)textual counterpoint at work in his writing. The very combination of title and subtitle illustrates a structure of poetic meaning as a structure of binary oppositions that underpins the text (others include Christian/classical, March/October, Demeter/Dionysus, heaven/underworld, Pre-Raphaelite/Raphaelite, knowing/not knowing, meaning/madness, etc.): *candidus* in Latin means "shining, bright, or white" (a link to Demeter as the Gravesean White Goddess), whereas *mystery* can mean shutting one's eyes. (*Candida* may also, of course, mean "candid or frank.")

Perhaps the most important connotation of the word *mystery* for the play is drawn from one of the most famous festivals in the ancient world: the Eleusinian Mysteries, which celebrate the mythical story of Demeter and her daughter Persephone (also known as Kore or as Proserpine to the Romans). Hades (or Pluto), lord of the underworld, seduces Persephone away to the world below, leaving her torchbearing mother desperately searching for her on the earth above. The text duly alludes, with a faint suggestion of ritual, to Demeter's torch in act II of the play, when Candida "comes in well aproned with a reading lamp." The Eleusinian Mysteries took place in the Greek month of Boedromion, our late September–early October, exactly when the play is set. Thus the text connects the festivals of both Dionysus and Demeter, a connection already made in the ancient myths and the celebrations themselves.

The figure of Persephone/Proserpine was very much in the air when Shaw wrote his play. As the independent daughter, she provided a role model for the women's movement at the end of the nineteenth century. That might well be why Shaw named Morell's secretary, the independent woman of her day, Proserpine Garnett. In fact, both her names allude to Persephone, whom Hades induced to eat the seeds of the pomegranate (from which Garnett is etymologically derived) to ensure her return to the underworld for part of each year. Swinburne, another possible model for Marchbanks, wrote two Proserpine poems in 1866, "The Garden of Proserpine" and "Hymn to Proserpine." The latter is narrated by a fourth-century Roman after the proclamation in Rome of Christianity as the new imperial religion, at the point of transition between the old gods and the new. The poet laureate Tennyson wrote his "Demeter and Persephone" in 1889. Most important, James Frazer's original edition of *The Golden Bough: A Study in Comparative Religion*, which was published in two volumes in 1890, interpreted the story of Demeter (or the Roman Ceres, goddess of corn) and Persephone as representing the passing of the seasons in the sowing, growing, and harvesting of the crops: winter when Proserpine resides in the underworld with Hades and the ground above is a barren "wasteland" (a trope found in the "droughte of March" from Chaucer's prologue to *The Canterbury Tales* as well as in T. S. Eliot's famous poem of that name); spring when Proserpine is released to the world above and new life is produced from an earth flowering with promise; and summer/harvesttime, associated with Demeter, when the earth is most fruitful. The Eleusinian Mysteries, a festival for initiates—not unlike Chaucer's pilgrims on their way to Canterbury or even modern pilgrims like Shaw attending Wagner's Bayreuth—were crucially concerned with understanding life, death, and regeneration. Moreover, the play takes place during the course of a single day, and Shaw's deliberate division of the acts into morning, afternoon, and night might serve as an analog of the passing not only of the seasons but also of a single life span.

When a third figure, Hecate or the crone (associated with the winter wasteland), is sometimes added to the mother-daughter combination of Demeter and Kore, they become known as the triple goddess; Shaw duly figures the crone in the Morells' off-stage, ironically named cook, Maria, and Candida jokingly refers to her fearful aspect when she talks about Eugene's "dread of Maria."

A lot of symbolic weight falls on the character of Candida, who must incarnate the divine mother of Western mythology, whether the Greek Demeter or Christian Mary, while remaining in some aspects a very ordinary, even philistine, late nineteenth-century middle-class Londoner. In the myths and in visual representations, Demeter and Persephone are often considered together as a mother-daughter dyad; Mrs. Warren and her daughter, Vivie, in Shaw's third play, *Mrs. Warren's Profession*, written the year before *Candida*, are a simpler playing out of this dyad. In *Candida*, however, aspects of both Demeter and Persephone are combined in the single character of Candida. Living in what the poet comes to understand as a domestic hell with her own particular lord of the underworld, Candida is a Persephone figure in her aspect as queen of that underworld. As such, Shaw—the onetime art critic—surely had in mind Dante Gabriel Rossetti's famous painting of Proserpine eating the pomegranate as a visual representation of Candida rather than "a brisk little woman" to whom he has given the name Proserpine. And Rossetti's painting of Demeter's daughter in the underworld functions as an implied visual counterpoint to Titian's *Assumption* of the mother of Christ heavenward. Such play with textual and figurative concepts, anticipating Freud's later use of the concepts of "displacement" and "condensation" to understand the logic of dreams, provides an interesting insight into Shaw's compositional method. Shaw even effects a structural or poetic irony with Candida as his version of Ibsen's Persephone figure, Nora in *A Doll's House*, for both in the myth and in Ibsen's play the wife manages to escape from husband and home as domestic hell—but not in Shaw's play.

A further play on the word *mystery* can be traced in the text by drawing on its etymological relation to the word *master*, which becomes one of the key words in act III: "James is master here. Don't you know that?" "By what right is he master?" "I don't know of any right that makes me master." "You don't know! . . . I wonder do you [Eugene] understand."[14] This thread culminates in Candida's declaration in her great speech at the end of the act: "I make him [her husband] master here." This theme also concerns the initiation of young Marchbanks into his poetic vocation, as he acquires self-mastery. And this mystery/master connotation has an additional dramatic resonance. Shaw's self-declared Pre-Raphaelite play evokes the mystery plays of the late Middle Ages, a period championed over the Renaissance by his great friend William Morris. The mysteries of fifteenth-century England, staged by the masters of trade guilds, were the focus of communal religious life, as were Greek drama and, in intention, Wagner's music-drama. In act I, the sometimes obtuse but always generous-minded Morell, already associated with the Guild of St. Matthew, recognizes Marchbanks's poetic knowledge as of a different order from his own: "You may be a master builder where I am only a humble journeyman."

Like a medieval craftsman, Shaw was producing his own masterpiece for initiation as a master dramatic poet. Some scholars have detected in *Candida* a parody of Chaucer's *Canterbury Tales*, itself a parody of codes of courtly honor and poetry often involving a triangle of husband, wife, and young lover. This should not surprise us, as Shaw, like W. B. Yeats, was at this time a frequent visitor to William Morris's home in Hammersmith, when Morris and his Kelmscott Press had already started printing his great work, the *Kelmscott Chaucer*.[15] Morris's wife, Jane, had been the favorite model for the Pre-Raphaelite painters, most famously for Rossetti in his *Proserpine*. That painting serves also as a textual reference for the dramatic narrative inasmuch as it expressed the artist-poet Rossetti's own desire for his muse, Jane Morris, the unhappily married wife of his friend. Further, Shaw seems to have learned from her in person that someone as beautiful and inspiring could be relatively commonplace—an aspect of Candida's character not always understood by "Candidamaniacs," as Shaw called them: "Rossetti's pictures . . . had driven [Mrs. Morris] into my consciousness as an imaginary figure. When she came into the room in her strangely beautiful garments . . . the effect was as if she had walked out of an Egyptian tomb at Luxor. Not until she had disposed herself more comfortably on the long couch opposite the settle did I compose myself into an acceptance of her as a real woman, and note that the wonderful curtain of hair was touched with gray, and the Rossetti face years older than it was in his pictures."[16] Again Shaw's way with names is significant: Candida *Morell* née *Burg*ess shares the first three letters of *both* her maiden and married names with Jane *Morris* née *Burden*.

When actors prepare a role, they learn the distinction between text and subtext. Readers, especially directors, of Shaw's plays need to distinguish between the text and its (inter)textuality. Shaw wove into the textual fabric of his plays detailed poetic structures drawing on as many strands of his culture as possible. The enduring popularity of *Candida* suggests that we should take seriously Shaw's evaluation of his own work. Shaw had written the part of Candida for Janet Achurch, the actress famous for playing Nora in Ibsen's *A Doll's House* and with whom he was in love. A few months after completing the play, on March 1, 1895, Shaw wrote a revealing letter, using terms familiar from this introduction, to Achurch's husband, who was Shaw's friend, an actor, and fellow Fabian Socialist Charles Charrington:

> I have not often formulated the lessons of my apprenticeship as a writer; but I did once write down in a notebook something like this: *You cannot be an artist until you have contracted yourself within the limits of your art.* Now the effect the artist produces is that of unlimitedness; and it is the great mystery and infinitude which attracts us all to art at first in these days. But when you get to practice an art you find that the unlimited length before you is

of exactly the same nature as the unlimited length before a horse in a circus. You start at the north end of the ring, and with immense galloping and jumping of hurdles you get to the south side. Call the north end Giotto; then the east end is Michel Angelo, beyond whom the course seems to stretch into the vastest eternity, exploring which, with your back turned on Giotto, for whose childish art you have an inconceivable contempt (which you had already acquired, perhaps, north east at Lippi and Botticelli) you push ahead, to find yourself presently in such a damnable bog of blathering unreality and manual clumsiness that you are glad to bear north again and come back Pre-Raphaelitically to Giotto again. And it is the same from Chaucer to Shakespear and on to Pope and back again in a hurry to Morris. . . . I have worked critically over quite enough of them to have formed an estimate of the merits, from the point of view of my own feeling of course, of the various points of the circle. I have my feeling for the exquisitely cultivated sense of beauty—an almost devotional sense—and the great pains and skill of execution which produces work of one kind, and for the bold ideas, the daring unscrupulous handling, the imaginative illusions that produce another kind. . . . When you see a man like me, trying to do fine counterpoint in even so few as three real parts, as in Candida, . . . never tell him he ought to go and write choruses instead.[17]

NOTES

1. When Shaw was asked where the Irish literary movement began, he replied jokingly "Bedford Park," a recently built middle-class London housing development that attracted such artistic and bohemian people as the Yeats family and Florence Farr. See *The Matter with Ireland* (2nd ed.) (Gainesville: University Press of Florida, 2001), 66.

2. *The Autobiography of William Butler Yeats* (London: Macmillan, 1944), 74.

3. In *Bernard Shaw: Collected Letters 1898–1910*, edited by Dan H. Laurence (London: Max Reinhardt, 1972), 461. To show that he did not take his "genius" too seriously, Shaw wrote an article,

"How to Become a Man of Genius," as he was completing the first draft of *Candida*, in which he typically deconstructed the whole notion, beginning ironically: "The secret at the bottom of the whole business is simply this: there is no such thing as a man of genius. I am a man of genius myself, and ought to know." In *Selected Non-Dramatic Writings of Bernard Shaw*, edited by Dan H. Laurence (Boston: Houghton Mifflin, 1965), 341.

4. The Morells' two children, Jimmy and Fluffy, who remain off-stage, have been staying in the country recovering from German measles with Candida and Eugene. The Socialist Shaw, well aware of the exploitation of child labor, did not write parts for child actors. The play's action only takes place because Candida decides to make a brief trip back home, with Eugene, to see how her husband is coping without her.

5. See Shaw's letter to H. G. Wells of December 4, 1922, *Selected Correspondence of Bernard Shaw: Bernard Shaw and H. G. Wells* (Toronto: University of Toronto Press, 1995), 117.

6. *The Masqueraders* featured Mrs. Patrick Campbell, who had just made a sensation in Arthur W. Pinero's *The Second Mrs. Tanqueray*, in the leading role of a woman bought and paid for in turns by her lover and her husband. Almost twenty years later, Shaw's infatuation with the actress, for whom he wrote *Pygmalion*, would nearly wreck his marriage.

7. At the beginning of Dionysia, a statue of the god was brought from its temple in Athens to the amphitheater, where it remained until the end of the festivities.

8. See Shaw's letter to James Huneker of April 6, 1904, *Bernard Shaw: Collected Letters 1898–1910*, edited by Dan H. Laurence (London: Max Reinhardt, 1972), 415.

9. See Martha Fodaski Black's *Shaw and Joyce: The Last Word in Stolentelling* (Gainesville: University Press of Florida, 1995).

10. In a letter to Ellen Terry of April 6, 1896, *Bernard Shaw: Collected Letters 1874–1897*, edited by Dan H. Laurence (London: Max Reinhardt, 1965), 623.

11. In a letter of March 16, 1895, to the American actor Richard Mansfield (due to play Marchbanks, but later withdrew from the part), Shaw himself makes the *Parsifal* connection: "The passage where you put your hand on your heart with a sympathetic sense of the stab Morell has suffered is cribbed from Wagner's *Parsifal*"; *Bernard Shaw: Collected Letters 1874–1897*, edited by Dan H. Laurence (London: Max Reinhardt, 1965), 499.

12. Shaw admitted another Christian Socialist clergyman, Stopford Brooke, to be a model for Morell in his play.

13. *Bernard Shaw's Letters to Trebitsch*, edited by Samuel A. Weiss (Stanford: Stanford University Press, 1986), 110.

14. *Mystery* is also synonymous with the word *secret*, which, as with *mad*, runs like a refrain or Wagnerian leitmotif through the text, along with almost ritual-like questions as to whether characters know or do not know, understand or do not understand.

15. The *Kelmscott Chaucer*, perhaps the most famous printed book of modern times, would be published in 1896, shortly before Morris died. Morris gave a copy to Shaw, an indication of Morris's estimation of the younger writer, who subsequently presented it to the great French sculptor Auguste Rodin.

16. *Shaw: An Autobiography 1856–1898*, selected from his writings by Stanley Weintraub (New York: Weybright and Talley, 1970), 159.

17. *Bernard Shaw: Collected Letters 1874–1897*, edited by Dan H. Laurence (London: Max Reinhardt, 1965), 490–91.

Suggestions for Further Reading

This "definitive" version of the text, originally published in *The Bodley Head Bernard Shaw Collected Plays with Prefaces, Volume I* (London: Max Reinhardt, 1970), is drawn from the latest version revised by Shaw himself for the Standard Edition (London: Constable, 1931–51). Perhaps the most important of earlier printed editions of the play is its original publication in the second volume of *Plays Pleasant and Unpleasant* (London: Grant Richards, 1898). *Candida & How He Lied to Her Husband: Facsimiles of the Holograph Manuscripts,* with an introduction by J. Percy Smith (New York: Garland, 1981), is a revealing facsimile of Shaw's longhand first draft with revisions.

Both *Bernard Shaw: The Diaries 1885–1897* (2 vols.), edited by Stanley Weintraub (University Park: Pennsylvania State University Press, 1986), and *Bernard Shaw: Collected Letters 1874–1897,* edited by Dan H. Laurence (London: Max Reinhardt, 1965), provide firsthand information on Shaw's life at the time he was writing *Candida*, while useful biographies of Shaw in this period include Margot Peters, *Bernard Shaw and the Actresses* (New York: Doubleday, 1980); Michael Holroyd, *Bernard Shaw: The Search for Love 1856–1898, Volume 1* (New York: Random House, 1988); and Sally Peters, *Bernard Shaw: The Ascent of the Superman* (New Haven: Yale University Press, 1996).

A great resource is *A Casebook on Candida*, edited by Stephen S. Stanton (New York: Crowell, 1962), which contains not only the text from the Standard Edition, but collects most of Shaw's miscellaneous comments on the play as well as background materials, criticism, and reviews. Included is Walter N. King's essay "The Rhetoric of 'Candida,'" which highlights the use of keywords in the text, originally published in *Modern Drama*, II (September 1959): 71–83. Margery Morgan's revealing chapter on *Candida* in *The Shavian Playground* (London: Methuen, 1967) continued King's emphasis, extending it to themes broached in the present introduction. Martin Meisel's indispensable study *Shaw and the Nineteenth Century Theater* (Princeton, NJ: Princeton University Press, 1963) fills in the background of the late nineteenth-century theatrical genres and models against which Shaw wrote his play. Louis Crompton's *Shaw the Dramatist* (Lincoln: University of Nebraska Press, 1969) highlights the context of the play in relation to Yeats and his play *The Land of Heart's Desire*, and points out that the mystery celebrated in the subtitle is, in fact, marriage.

Barbara Bellow Watson offers a favorable feminist reading in *A Shavian Guide to the Intelligent Woman* (New York: Norton, 1972), while J. Ellen Gainor contributes a somewhat negative feminist interpretation in *Shaw's Daughters: Dramatic and Narrative Constructions of Gender* (Ann Arbor: University of Michigan Press, 1991). Gainor does, however, stress the importance of Prossy as the new woman to the play and, while failing to see that Candida herself is a Proserpine figure, opens the door to Shaw's compositional method highlighted here with the phrase "Shaw's matrix of inverted allusions." Tracy C. Davis's "Shaw's Interstices of Empire: Decolonizing at Home and Abroad" in the useful *Cambridge Guide to George Bernard Shaw*, edited by Christopher Innes (Cambridge: Cambridge University Press, 1998), widens the feminist argument to the colonialist context by drawing attention to "Shaw's ability to relate the microeconomy and power of a household to the macroeconomic concerns of global capitalism, its product (colonialism), and the complicity of colonialism in gender ideology and racism."

Many articles on Candida can be found in *SHAW: The Annual of Bernard Shaw Studies* (University Park: Pennsylvania State University Press, 1980–). Patrick White's "Chaucer: *Franklin's Tale* as analogue for *Candida*," in *SHAW* 12 (1992): 213–28, explores the Chaucer connections.

Preface

In the autumn of 1894 I spent a few weeks in Florence, where I occupied myself with the religious art of the Middle Ages and its destruction by the Renascence. From a former visit to Italy on the same business I had hurried back to Birmingham to discharge my duties as musical critic at the Festival there. On that occasion a very remarkable collection of the works of our British "pre-Raphaelite" painters was on view. I looked at these, and then went into the Birmingham churches to see the windows of William Morris and Burne-Jones. On the whole, Birmingham was more hopeful than the Italian cities; for the art it had to shew me was the work of living men, whereas modern Italy had, as far as I could see, no more connection with Giotto than Port Said has with Ptolemy. Now I am no believer in the worth of any mere taste for art that cannot produce what it professes to appreciate. When my subsequent visit to Italy found me practising the playwright's craft, the time was ripe for a modern pre-Raphaelite play. Religion was alive again, coming back upon men, even upon clergymen, with such power that not the Church of England itself could keep it out. Here my activity as a Socialist had placed me on sure and familiar ground. To me the members of the Guild of St Matthew were no more "High Church clergymen," Dr Clifford no more "an eminent Nonconformist divine," than I was to them "an infidel." There is only one religion, though there are a hundred versions of it. We all had the same thing to say; and though some of us cleared our throats to say it by singing revolutionary lyrics and republican hymns, we thought nothing of singing them to the music of Sullivan's Onward Christian Soldiers or Haydn's God Preserve the Emperor.

Now unity, however desirable in political agitations, is fatal to drama; for every drama must present a conflict. The end may be reconciliation or destruction; or, as in life itself, there may be no end; but the conflict is indispensable: no conflict, no drama. Certainly it is easy to dramatize the prosaic conflict of Christian Socialism with vulgar Unsocialism: for instance, in Widowers' Houses, the clergyman, who does not appear on the stage at all, is the real antagonist of the slum landlord. But the obvious conflicts of unmistakeable good with unmistakeable evil can only supply the crude drama of villain and hero, in which some absolute point of view is taken, and the dissentients are treated by the dramatist as enemies to be piously glorified or indignantly vilified. In such cheap wares I do not deal. Even in my unpleasant propagandist plays I have allowed every person his or her own point of view, and I have, I hope, to the full extent of my understanding of him, been as sympathetic with Sir George Crofts as with any of the more genial and popular characters in the present volume. To distil the quintessential drama from pre-Raphaelitism, medieval or modern, it must be shewn at its best in conflict with the first broken, nervous, stumbling attempts to formulate its own revolt against itself as it develops into something higher. A coherent explanation of any such revolt, addressed intelligibly and prosaically to the intellect, can only come when the work is done, and indeed *done with*: that is to say, when the development, accomplished, admitted, and assimilated, is a story of yesterday. Long before any such understanding can be reached, the eyes of men begin to turn towards the distant light of the new age. Discernible at first only by the eyes of the man of genius, it must be focussed by him on the speculum of a work of art, and flashed back from that into the eyes of the common man. Nay, the artist himself has no other way of making himself conscious of the ray: it is by a blind instinct that he keeps on building up his masterpieces until their pinnacles catch the glint of the unrisen sun. Ask him to explain himself prosaically, and you find that he "writes like an angel and talks like poor Poll," and is himself the first to make that epigram at his own expense. John Ruskin has told us clearly enough what is in the pictures of Carpaccio and Bellini: let him explain, if he can, where we shall be when the sun that is caught by the summits of the work of his favorite Tintoretto, of his aversion Rembrandt, of Mozart, of Beethoven and Wagner, of Blake and of Shelley, shall have reached the valleys. Let Ibsen explain, if he can, why the building of churches and happy homes is not the ultimate destiny of Man, and why, to thrill the unsatisifed younger generations, he must mount beyond it to heights that now seem unspeakably giddy and dreadful to him, and from which the first climbers must fall and dash themselves to pieces. He cannot explain it: he can only shew it to you as a vision in the magic glass of his artwork; so that you may catch his presentiment and make what you can of it. And this is the function that raises dramatic art above imposture and pleasure hunting, and enables the playwright to be something more than a skilled liar and pandar.

Here, then, was the higher but vaguer and timider vision, the incoherent, mischievous, and even ridiculous unpracticalness, which offered me a dramatic antagonist for the clear, bold, sure, sensible, benevolent, salutarily shortsighted Christian Socialist idealism. I availed myself of it in Candida, the drunken scene in which has been much appreciated, I am told, in Aberdeen. I purposely contrived the play in such a way as to make the expenses of representations insignificant; so that, without pretending that I could appeal to a very wide circle of playgoers, I could reasonably sound a few of our more enlightened managers as to an experiment with half a dozen afternoon performances. They admired the play generously: indeed I think that if any of them had been young enough to play the poet, my proposal might have been acceded to, in spite of many incidental difficulties. Nay, if only I had made the poet a cripple, or at least blind, so as to combine an easier disguise with a larger claim for sympathy, something might have been done. Richard Mansfield, who had, with apparent ease, made me quite famous in America by his production of my plays, went so far as to put the play actually into rehearsal before he would confess himself beaten by the physical difficulties of the part. But they did beat him; and Candida did not see the footlights until my old ally the Independent Theatre, making a propagandist tour through the provinces with A Doll's House, added Candida to its repertory, to the great astonishment of its audiences.

Candida

ACT I

A fine morning in October 1894 in the north east quarter
of London, a vast district miles away from the London of May-
fair and St James's, and much less narrow, squalid, fetid and
airless in its slums. It is strong in unfashionable middle class
life: wide-streeted; myriad-populated; well served with ugly
iron urinals, Radical clubs, and tram lines carrying a perpet-
ual stream of yellow cars; enjoying in its main thoroughfares
the luxury of grass-grown "front gardens" untrodden by the
foot of man save as to the path from the gate to the hall
door; blighted by a callously endured monotony of miles and
miles of unlovely brick houses, black iron railings, stony
pavements, slated roofs, and respectably ill dressed or dis-
reputably worse dressed people, quite accustomed to the
place, and mostly plodding uninterestedly about somebody
else's work. The little energy and eagerness that crop up
shew themselves in cockney cupidity and business "push."
Even the policemen and the chapels are not infrequent
enough to break the monotony. The sun is shining cheerfully:
there is no fog; and though the smoke effectually prevents
anything, whether faces and hands or bricks and mortar,
from looking fresh and clean; it is not hanging heavily
enough to trouble a Londoner.

This desert of unattractiveness has its oasis. Near the outer
end of the Hackney Road is a park of 217 acres, fenced in,
not by railings, but by a wooden paling, and containing
plenty of greensward, trees, a lake for bathers, flower beds
which are triumphs of the admired cockney art of carpet gar-
dening, and a sandpit, originally imported from the seaside

for the delight of children, but speedily deserted on its becoming a natural vermin preserve for all the petty fauna of Kingsland, Hackney, and Hoxton. A bandstand, an unfurnished forum for religious, anti-religious, and political orators, cricket pitches, a gymnasium, and an old fashioned stone kiosk are among its attractions. Wherever the prospect is bounded by trees or rising green grounds, it is a pleasant place. Where the ground stretches flat to the grey palings, with bricks and mortar, sky signs, crowded chimneys and smoke beyond, the prospect makes it desolate and sordid.

The best view of Victoria Park is commanded by the front window of St Dominic's Parsonage, from which not a brick is visible. The parsonage is semi-detached, with a front garden and a porch. Visitors go up the flight of steps to the porch: tradespeople and members of the family go down by a door under the steps to the basement, with a breakfast room, used for all meals, in front, and the kitchen at the back. Upstairs, on the level of the hall door, is the drawingroom, with its large plate glass window looking out on the park. In this, the only sitting room that can be spared from the children and the family meals, the parson, the Reverend James Mavor Morell, does his work. He is sitting in a strong round backed revolving chair at the end of a long table, which stands across the window, so that he can cheer himself with a view of the park over his left shoulder. At the opposite end of the table, adjoining it, is a little table only half as wide as the other, with a typewriter on it. His typist is sitting at this machine, with her back to the window. The large table is littered with pamphlets, journals, letters, nests of drawers, an office diary, postage scales and the like. A spare chair for visitors having business with the parson is in the middle, turned to his end. Within reach of his hand is a stationery case, and a photograph in a frame. The wall behind him is fitted with bookshelves, on which an adept eye can measure the parson's casuistry and divinity by Maurice's Theological Essays and a complete set of Browning's poems, and the reformer's politics by a yellow backed Progress and Poverty, Fabian Essays, A Dream of John Ball, Marx's Cap-

ital, and half a dozen other literary landmarks in Socialism.
Facing him on the other side of the room, near the typewriter, is the door. Further down opposite the fireplace, a
bookcase stands on a cellaret, with a sofa near it. There is a
generous fire burning; and the hearth, with a comfortable
armchair and a black japanned flower-painted coal scuttle at
one side, a miniature chair for children on the other, a var-
nished wooden mantelpiece, with neatly moulded shelves,
tiny bits of mirror let into the panels, a travelling clock in a
leather case (the inevitable wedding present), and on the wall
above a large autotype of the chief figure in Titian's Assumption of the Virgin, is very inviting. Altogether the room is the
room of a good housekeeper, vanquished, as far as the table
is concerned, by an untidy man, but elsewhere mistress of the
situation. The furniture, in its ornamental aspect, betrays the
style of the advertized "drawingroom suite" of the pushing
suburban furniture dealer; but there is nothing useless or
pretentious in the room, money being too scarce in the house
of an east end parson to be wasted on snobbish trimmings.

The Reverend James Mavor Morell is a Christian Socialist
clergyman of the Church of England, and an active member
of the Guild of St Matthew and the Christian Social Union.
A vigorous, genial, popular man of forty, robust and good-
looking, full of energy, with pleasant, hearty, considerate
manners, and a sound unaffected voice, which he uses with a
clean athletic articulation of a practised orator, and with a
wide range and perfect command of expression. He is a first
rate clergyman, able to say what he likes to whom he likes,
to lecture people without setting himself up against them, to
impose his authority on them without humiliating them,
and, on occasion, to interfere in their business without im-
pertinence. His well-spring of enthusiasm and sympathetic
emotion has never run dry for a moment: he still eats and
sleeps heartily enough to win the daily battle between ex-
haustion and recuperation triumphantly. Withal, a great
baby, pardonably vain of his powers and unconsciously
pleased with himself. He has a healthy complexion: good
forehead, with the brows somewhat blunt, and the eyes

*bright and eager, mouth resolute but not particularly well cut,
and a substantial nose, with the mobile spreading nostrils of
the dramatic orator, void, like all his features, of subtlety.*

*The typist, Miss Proserpine Garnett, is a brisk little
woman of about 30, of the lower middle class, neatly but
cheaply dressed in a black merino skirt and a blouse, notably
pert and quick of speech, and not very civil in her manner,
but sensitive and affectionate. She is clattering away busily at
her machine whilst Morell opens the last of his morning's letters. He realizes its contents with a comic groan of despair.*

PROSERPINE: Another lecture?

MORELL: Yes. The Hoxton Freedom Group want me to ad-
dress them on Sunday morning [*he lays great emphasis on
Sunday, this being the unreasonable part of the business*].
What are they?

PROSERPINE: Communist Anarchists, I think.

MORELL: Just like Anarchists not to know that they cant have
a parson on Sunday! Tell them to come to church if they
want to hear me: it will do them good. Say I can come on
Mondays and Thursdays only. Have you the diary there?

PROSERPINE [*taking up the diary*] Yes.

MORELL: Have I any lecture on for next Monday?

PROSERPINE [*referring to the diary*] Tower Hamlets Radical
Club.

MORELL: Well, Thursday then?

PROSERPINE: English Land Restoration League.

MORELL: What next?

PROSERPINE: Guild of St Matthew on Monday. Independent
Labor Party, Greenwich Branch, on Thursday. Monday, Social-
Democratic Federation, Mile End Branch. Thursday, first
Confirmation class. [*Impatiently*] Oh, I'd better tell them
you can't come. Theyre only half a dozen ignorant and con-
ceited costermongers without five shillings between them.

MORELL [*amused*] Ah; but you see theyre near relatives of
mine.

PROSERPINE [*staring at him*] Relatives of yours!

MORELL: Yes: we have the same father—in Heaven.

PROSERPINE [*relieved*] Oh, is that all?

MORELL [*with a sadness which is a luxury to a man whose voice expresses it so finely*] Ah, you dont believe it. Everybody says it: nobody believes it: nobody. [*Briskly, getting back to business*] Well, well! Come, Miss Proserpine: cant you find a date for the costers? what about the 25th? That was vacant the day before yesterday.

PROSERPINE [*referring to diary*] Engaged. The Fabian Society.

MORELL: Bother the Fabian Society! Is the 28th gone too?

PROSERPINE: City dinner. Youre invited to dine with the Founders' Company.

MORELL: Thatll do: I'll go to the Hoxton Group of Freedom instead. [*She enters the engagement in silence, with implacable disparagement of the Hoxton Anarchists in every line of her face. Morell bursts open the cover of a copy of The Church Reformer, which has come by post, and glances through Mr Stewart Headlam's leader and the Guild of St Matthew news. These proceedings are presently enlivened by the appearance of Morell's curate, the Reverend Alexander Mill, a young gentleman gathered by Morell from the nearest University settlement, whither he had come from Oxford to give the east end of London the benefit of his university training. He is a conceitedly well intentioned, enthusiastic, immature novice, with nothing positively unbearable about him except a habit of speaking with his lips carefully closed a full half inch from each corner for the sake of a finicking articulation and a set of university vowels, this being his chief means so far of bringing his Oxford refinement (as he calls his habits) to bear on Hackney vulgarity. Morell, whom he has won over by a doglike devotion, looks up indulgently from The Church Reformer, and remarks*] Well, Lexy? Late again, as usual!

LEXY: I'm afraid so. I wish I could get up in the morning.

MORELL [*exulting in his own energy*] Ha! ha! [*Whimsically*] Watch and pray, Lexy: watch and pray.

LEXY: I know. [*Rising wittily to the occasion*] But how can I watch and pray when I am asleep? Isnt that so, Miss Prossy? [*He makes for the warmth of the fire*].

PROSERPINE [*sharply*] Miss Garnett, if you please.

LEXY: I beg your pardon. Miss Garnett.

PROSERPINE: Youve got to do all the work today.

LEXY [*on the hearth*] Why?

PROSERPINE: Never mind why. It will do you good to earn your supper before you eat it, for once in a way, as I do. Come! dont dawdle. You should have been off on your rounds half an hour ago.

LEXY [*perplexed*] Is she in earnest, Morell?

MORELL [*in the highest spirits: his eyes dancing*] Yes. I am going to dawdle today.

LEXY: You! You dont know how.

MORELL [*rising*] Ha! ha! Don't I? I'm going to have this morning all to myself. My wife's coming back: she's due here at 11.45.

LEXY [*surprised*] Coming back already! with the children? I thought they were going to stay to the end of the month.

MORELL: So they are: she's only coming up for two days, to get some flannel things for Jimmy, and to see how we're getting on without her.

LEXY [*anxiously*] But, my dear Morell, if what Jimmy and Fluffy had was scarlatina, do you think it wise—

MORELL: Scarlatina! Rubbish! it was German measles. I brought it into the house myself from the Pycroft Street school. A parson is like a doctor, my boy: he must face infection as a soldier must face bullets. [*He claps Lexy manfully on the shoulders*]. Catch the measles if you can, Lexy: she'll nurse you; and what a piece of luck that will be for you! Eh?

LEXY [*smiling uneasily*] It's so hard to understand you about Mrs Morell—

MORELL [*tenderly*] Ah, my boy, get married: get married to a good woman; and then youll understand. Thats a foretaste of what will be best in the Kingdom of Heaven we are trying to establish on earth. That will cure you of dawdling. An honest man feels that he must pay Heaven for every hour of happiness with a good spell of hard unselfish work to make others happy. We have no more right to consume happiness without producing it than to consume wealth without producing it. Get a wife like my Candida; and youll always be in arrear with your repayment. [*He pats Lexy affectionately and moves to leave the room*].

LEXY: Oh, wait a bit: I forgot. [*Morell halts and turns with the door knob in his hand*]. Your father-in-law is coming round to see you.

Morell, surprised and not pleased, shuts the door again, with a complete change of manner.

MORELL: Mr Burgess?

LEXY: Yes. I passed him in the park, arguing with somebody. He asked me to let you know that he was coming.

MORELL [*half incredulous*] But he hasnt called here for three years. Are you sure, Lexy? Youre not joking, are you?

LEXY [*earnestly*] No sir, really.

MORELL [*thoughtfully*] Hm! Time for him to take another look at Candida before she grows out of his knowledge. [*He resigns himself to the inevitable, and goes out*].

Lexy looks after him with beaming worship. Miss Garnett, not being able to shake Lexy, relieves her feelings by worrying the typewriter.

LEXY: What a good man! What a thorough loving soul he is! [*He takes Morell's place at the table, making himself very comfortable as he takes out a cigaret*].

PROSERPINE [*impatiently, pulling the letter she has been working at off the typewriter and folding it*] Oh, a man ought to be able to be fond of his wife without making a fool of himself about her.

LEXY [*shocked*] Oh, Miss Prossy!

PROSERPINE [*snatching at the stationery case for an envelope, in which she encloses the letter as she speaks*] Candida here, and Candida there, and Candida everywhere! [*She licks the envelope*]. It's enough to drive anyone out of their senses [*thumping the envelope to make it stick*] to hear a woman raved about in that absurd manner merely because she's got good hair and a tolerable figure.

LEXY [*with reproachful gravity*] I think her extremely beautiful, Miss Garnett. [*He takes the photograph up; looks at it; and adds, with even greater impressiveness*] extremely beautiful. How fine her eyes are!

PROSERPINE: Her eyes are not a bit better than mine: now! [*He puts down the photograph and stares austerely at her*]. And you know very well you think me dowdy and second rate enough.

LEXY [*rising majestically*] Heaven forbid that I should think of any of God's creatures in such a way! [*He moves stiffly away from her across the room to the neighborhood of the bookcase*].

PROSERPINE [*sarcastically*] Thank you. Thats very nice and comforting.

LEXY [*saddened by her depravity*] I had no idea you had any feelings against Mrs Morell.

PROSERPINE [*indignantly*] I have no feeling against her. She's very nice, very good-hearted: I'm very fond of her, and can appreciate her real qualities far better than any man can. [*He shakes his head sadly. She rises and comes at him with intense pepperiness*]. You dont believe me? You think I'm jealous? Oh, what a knowledge of the human heart you have, Mr Lexy Mill! How well you know the weaknesses of Woman, dont you? It must be so nice to be a man and have a fine penetrating intellect instead of mere emotions like us, and to know that the reason we dont share your amorous delusions is that we're all jealous of one another! [*She abandons him with a toss of her shoulders, and crosses to the fire to warm her hands*].

LEXY: Ah, if you women only had the same clue to Man's strength that you have to his weakness, Miss Prossy, there would be no Woman Question.

PROSERPINE [*over her shoulder, as she stoops, holding her hands to the blaze*] Where did you hear Morell say that? You didnt invent it yourself: youre not clever enough.

LEXY: Thats quite true. I am not ashamed of owing him that, as I owe him so many other spiritual truths. He said it at the annual conference of the Women's Liberal Federation. Allow me to add that though they didnt appreciate it, I, a mere man, did. [*He turns to the bookcase again, hoping that this may leave her crushed*].

PROSERPINE [*putting her hair straight at a panel of mirror in*

the mantelpiece] Well, when you talk to me, give me your
own ideas, such as they are, and not his. You never cut a
poorer figure than when you are trying to imitate him.

LEXY [*stung*] I try to follow his example, not to imitate him.

PROSERPINE [*coming at him again on her way back to her
work*] Yes, you do: you imitate him. Why do you tuck your
umbrella under your left arm instead of carrying it in your
hand like anyone else? Why do you walk with your chin
stuck out before you, hurrying along with that eager look in
your eyes? you! who never get up before half past nine in the
morning. Why do you say "knoaledge" in church, though
you always say "knolledge" in private conversation! Bah! do
you think I dont know? [*She goes back to the typewriter*].
Here! come and set about your work: weve wasted enough
time for one morning. Here's a copy of the diary for today.
[*She hands him a memorandum*].

LEXY [*deeply offended*] Thank you. [*He takes it and stands at
the table with his back to her, reading it. She begins to tran-
scribe her shorthand notes on the typewriter without trou-
bling herself about his feelings*].

*The door opens; and Mr Burgess enters unannounced. He
is a man of sixty, made coarse and sordid by the compulsory
selfishness of petty commerce, and later on softened into
sluggish bumptiousness by overfeeding and commercial suc-
cess. A vulgar ignorant guzzling man, offensive and contemptuous to people whose labor is cheap, respectful to
wealth and rank, and quite sincere without rancor or envy in
both attitudes. The world has offered him no decently paid
work except that of a sweater; and he has become, in conse-
quence, somewhat hoggish. But he has no suspicion of this
himself, and honestly regards his commercial prosperity as
the inevitable and socially wholesome triumph of the ability,
industry, shrewdness, and experience in business of a man
who in private is easygoing, affectionate, and humorously
convivial to a fault. Corporeally he is podgy, with a snoutish
nose in the centre of a flat square face, a dust colored beard
with a patch of grey in the centre under his chin, and small
watery blue eyes with a plaintively sentimental expression,*

which he transfers easily to his voice by his habit of pompously intoning his sentences.

BURGESS [*stopping on the threshold, and looking around*] They told me Mr Morell was here.

PROSERPINE [*rising*] I'll fetch him for you.

BURGESS [*staring disappointedly at her*] Youre not the same young lady as hused to typewrite for him?

PROSERPINE: No.

BURGESS [*grumbling on his way to the hearth-rug*] No: she was young-er. [*Miss Garnett stares at him; then goes out, slamming the door*]. Startin on your rounds, Mr Mill?

LEXY [*folding his memorandum and pocketing it*] Yes: I must be off presently.

BURGESS [*momentously*] Dont let me detain you, Mr Mill. What I come about is private between me and Mr Morell.

LEXY [*huffily*] I have no intention of intruding, I am sure, Mr Burgess. Good morning.

BURGESS [*patronizingly*] Oh, good morning to you.

Morell returns as Lexy is making for the door.

MORELL [*to Lexy*] Off to work?

LEXY: Yes, sir.

MORELL: Take my silk handkerchief and wrap your throat up. Theres a cold wind. Away with you.

Lexy, more than consoled for Burgess's rudeness, brightens up and goes out.

BURGESS: Spoilin your korates as usu'l, James. Good mornin. When I pay a man, an' 'is livin depens on me, I keep him in 'is place.

MORELL [*rather shortly*] I always keep my curates in their places as my helpers and comrades. If you get as much work out of your clerks and warehousemen as I do out of my curates, you must be getting rich pretty fast. Will you take your old chair?

He points with curt authority to the armchair beside the fireplace; then takes the spare chair from the table and sits down at an unfamiliar distance from his visitor.

BURGESS [*without moving*] Just the same as hever, James!

MORELL: When you last called—it was about three years ago,

I think—you said the same thing a little more frankly. Your exact words then were "Just as big a fool as ever, James!"

BURGESS [*soothingly*] Well, praps I did; but [*with conciliatory cheerfulness*] I meant no hoffence by it. A clorgyman is privileged to be a bit of a fool, you know: it's ony becomin in 'is profession that he should. Anyhow, I come here, not to rake up hold differences, but to let bygones be bygones. [*Suddenly becoming very solemn, and approaching Morell*] James: three years ago, you done me a hil turn. You done me hout of a contrac; an when I gev you arsh words in my natral disappointment, you turned my daughrter again me. Well, Ive come to hact the part of a Kerischin. [*Offering his hand*] I forgive you, James.

MORELL [*starting up*] Confound your impudence!

BURGESS [*retreating, with almost lachrymose deprecation of his treatment*] Is that becomin language for a clorgyman, James? And you so particlar, too!

MORELL [*hotly*] No, sir: it is not becoming language for a clergyman. I used the wrong word. I should have said damn your impudence: thats what St Paul or any honest priest would have said to you. Do you think I have forgotten that tender of yours for the contract to supply clothing to the workhouse?

BURGESS [*in a paroxysm of public spirit*] I hacted in the hinterest of the ratepayers, James. It was the lowest tender: you carnt deny that.

MORELL: Yes, the lowest, becuase you paid worse wages than any other employer—starvation wages—aye, worse than starvation wages—to the women who made the clothing. Your wages would have driven them to the streets to keep body and soul together. [*Getting angrier and angrier*] Those women were my parishioners. I shamed the Guardians out of accepting your tender: I shamed the ratepayers out of letting them do it: I shamed everybody but you. [*Boiling over*] How dare you, sir, come here and offer to forgive me, and talk about your daughter, and—

BURGESS: Heasy, James! heasy! heasy! Dont git hinto a fluster about nothink. Ive howned I was wrong.

MORELL: Have you? I didnt hear you.

BURGESS: Of course I did. I hown it now. Come: I harsk your pardon for the letter I wrote you. Is that enough?

MORELL [*snapping his fingers*] Thats nothing. Have you raised the wages?

BURGESS [*triumphantly*] Yes.

MORELL: What!

BURGESS [*unctuously*] Ive turned a moddle hemployer. I dont hemploy no women now: theyre all sacked; and the work is done by machinery. Not a man 'as less than six-pence a *h*our; and the skilled ands gits the Trade Union rate. [*Proudly*] What ave you to say to me now?

MORELL [*overwhelmed*] Is it possible! Well, theres more joy in heaven over one sinner that repenteth!—[*Going to Burgess with an explosion of apologetic cordiality*] My dear Burgess: how splendid of you! I most heartily beg your pardon for my hard thoughts. [*Grasping his hand*] And now, dont you feel the better for the change? Come! confess! youre happier. You look happier.

BURGESS [*ruefully*] Well, praps I do. I spose I must, since you notice it. At all events, I git my contrax assepted by the County Council. [*Savagely*] They dussent ave nothink to do with me unless I paid fair wages: curse em for a parcel o meddlin fools!

MORELL [*dropping his hand, utterly discouraged*] So that was why you raised the wages! [*He sits down moodily*].

BURGESS [*severely, in spreading, mounting tones*] Woy helse should I do it? What does it lead to but drink and huppish-ness in workin men? [*He seats himself magisterially in the easy chair*]. It's hall very well for you, James: it gits you hinto the papers and makes a great man of you; but you never think of the arm you do, puttin money into the pockets of workin men that they dunno ow to spend, and takin it from people that might be makin a good huse on it.

MORELL [*with a heavy sigh, speaking with cold politeness*] What is your business with me this morning? I shall not pre-tend to believe that you are here merely out of family senti-ment.

BURGESS [*obstinately*] Yes I ham: just family sentiment and nothink helse.

MORELL [*with weary calm*] I dont believe you.

BURGESS [*rising threateningly*] Dont say that to me again, James Mavor Morell.

MORELL [*unmoved*] I'll say it just as often as may be necessary to convince you that it's true. I dont believe you.

BURGESS [*collapsing into an abyss of wounded feeling*] Oh, well, if youre detormined to be hunfriendly, I spose I'd better go. [*He moves reluctantly towards the door. Morell makes no sign. He lingers*]. I didnt hexpect to find a hunforgivin spirit in you, James. [*Morell still not responding, he takes a few more reluctant steps doorwards. Then he comes back, whining*]. We huseter git on well enough, spite of our different hopinions. Woy are you so changed to me? I give you my word I come here in peeorr [pure] frenliness, not wishin to be hon bad terms with my hown daughrter's usban. Come, James: be a Kerischin, and shake ands. [*He puts his hand sentimentally on Morell's shoulder.*]

MORELL [*looking up at him thoughtfully*] Look here, Burgess. Do you want to be as welcome here as you were before you lost that contract?

BURGESS: I do, James. I do—*h*onest.

MORELL: Then why dont you behave as you did then?

BURGESS [*cautiously removing his hand*] Ow d'y'mean?

MORELL: I'll tell you. You thought me a young fool then.

BURGESS [*coaxingly*] No I didnt, James. I—

MORELL [*cutting him short*] Yes, you did. And I thought you an old scoundrel.

BURGESS [*most vehemently deprecating this gross self-accusation on Morell's part*] No you didnt, James. Now you do yourself a hinjustice.

MORELL: Yes I did. Well, that did not prevent our getting on very well together. God made you what I call a scoundrel as He made me what you call a fool. [*The effect of this observation on Burgess is to remove the keystone of his moral arch. He becomes bodily weak, and, with his eyes fixed on Morell in a helpless stare, puts out his hand apprehensively*

to balance himself, as if the floor had suddenly sloped
under him. Morell proceeds, in the same tone of quiet con-
viction] It was not for me to quarrel with His handiwork
in the one case more than in the other. So long as you come
here honestly as a self-respecting, thorough, convinced
scoundrel, justifying your scoundrelism and proud of it, you
are welcome. But [and now Morell's tone becomes formi-
dable; and he rises and strikes the back of the chair for
greater emphasis] I wont have you here snivelling about being a model employer and a converted man when youre only
an apostate with your coat turned for the sake of a County
Council contract. [He nods at him to enforce the point; then
goes to the hearth-rug, where he takes up a comfortably
commanding position with his back to the fire, and contin-
ues] No: I like a man to be true to himself, even in wicked-
ness. Come now: either take your hat and go; or else sit
down and give me a good scoundrelly reason for wanting to
be friends with me. [Burgess, whose emotions have subsided
sufficiently to be expressed by a dazed grin, is relieved by this
concrete proposition. He ponders it for a moment, and then,
slowly and very modestly, sits down in the chair Morell has
just left]. Thats right. Now out with it.

BURGESS [chuckling in spite of himself] Well, you orr a queer
bird, James, and no mistake. But [almost enthusiastically]
one carnt elp likin you: besides, as I said afore, of course one
dont take hall a clorgyman says seriously, or the world
couldnt go on. Could it now? [He composes himself for
graver discourse, and, turning his eyes on Morell, proceeds
with dull seriousness] Well, I dont mind tellin you, since it's
your wish we should be free with one another, that I did
think you a bit of a fool once; but I'm beginnin to think that
praps I was be'ind the times a bit.

MORELL [exultant] Aha! Youre finding that out at last, are you?

BURGESS [portentously] Yes: times 'as changed mor'n I could
a believed. Five yorr [year] ago, no sensible man would a
thought o takin hup with your hidears. I hused to wonder
you was let preach at all. Why, I know a clorgyman what 'as
bin kep hout of his job for yorrs by the Bishop o London, al-

though the pore feller's not a bit more religious than you are.
But today, if hennyone was to horffer to bet me a thousan
poun that youll hend by bein a bishop yourself, I dussent
take the bet. [*Very impressively*] You and your crew are git-
tin hinfluential: I can see that. Theyll ave to give you some-
think someday, if it's honly to stop your mouth. You ad the
right instinc arter all, James: the line you took is the payin
line in the long run for a man o your sort.

MORELL [*offering his hand with thorough decision*] Shake
hands, Burgess. Now youre talking honestly. I dont think
theyll make me a bishop; but if they do, I'll introduce you to
the biggest jobbers I can get to come to my dinner parties.

BURGESS [*who has risen with a sheepish grin and accepted the
hand of friendship*] You will ave your joke, James. Our quarrel's made up now, aint it?

A WOMAN'S VOICE: Say yes, James.

*Startled, they turn quickly and find that Candida has just
come in, and is looking at them with an amused maternal indulgence which is her characteristic expression. She is a
woman of 33, well built, well nourished, likely, one guesses, to
become matronly later on, but now quite at her best, with the
double charm of youth and motherhood. Her ways are those
of a woman who has found that she can always manage
people by engaging their affection, and who does so frankly
and instinctively without the smallest scruple. So far, she is like
any other pretty woman who is just clever enough to make the
most of her sexual attractions for trivially selfish ends; but
Candida's serene brow, courageous eyes, and well set mouth
and chin signify largeness of mind and dignity of character to
ennoble her cunning in the affections. A wise-hearted observer,
looking at her, would at once guess that whoever had placed
the Virgin of the Assumption over her hearth did so because he
fancied some spiritual resemblance between them, and yet
would not suspect either her husband or herself of any such
idea, or indeed of any concern with the art of Titian.*

*Just now she is in bonnet and mantle, carrying a strapped
rug with her umbrella stuck through it, a handbag, and a
supply of illustrated papers.*

MORELL [*shocked at his remissness*] Candida! Why—[*he looks at his watch, and is horrified to find it so late*]. My darling! [*Hurrying to her and seizing the rug strap, pouring forth his remorseful regrets all the time*] I intended to meet you at the train. I let the time slip. [*Flinging the rug on the sofa*] I was so engrossed by—[*returning to her*]—I forgot—oh! [*He embraces her with penitent emotion*].

BURGESS [*a little shamefaced and doubtful of his reception*] How orr you, Candy? [*She, still in Morell's arms, offers him her cheek, which he kisses*]. James and me is come to a nunnerstannin. A honorable unnerstannin. Ain we, James?

MORELL [*impetuously*] Oh bother your understanding! youve kept me late for Candida. [*With compassionate fervor*] My poor love: how did you manage about the luggage? How—

CANDIDA [*stopping him and disengaging herself*] There! there! there! I wasnt alone. Eugene has been down with us; and we travelled together.

MORELL [*pleased*] Eugene!

CANDIDA: Yes: he's struggling with my luggage, poor boy. Go out, dear, at once; or he'll pay for the cab; and I dont want that [*Morell hurries out. Candida puts down her handbag; then takes off her mantle and bonnet and puts them on the sofa with the rug, chatting meanwhile*]. Well, papa: how are you getting on at home?

BURGESS: The ouse aint worth livin in since you left it, Candy. I wish youd come round and give the gurl a talkin to. Who's this Eugene that comes with you?

CANDIDA: Oh, Eugene's one of James's discoveries. He found him sleeping on the Embankment last June. Havnt you noticed our new picture [*pointing to the Virgin*]? He gave us that.

BURGESS [*incredulously*] Garn! D'you mean to tell me—your hown father!—that cab touts or such like, orf the Embankment, buys pictures like that? [*Severely*] Dont deceive me, Candy: it's a 'Igh Church picture; and James chose it hisself.

CANDIDA: Guess again. Eugene isnt a cab tout.

BURGESS: Then what is he? [*Sarcastically*] A nobleman, I spose.

CANDIDA [*nodding delightedly*] Yes. His uncle's a peer! A real live earl.

BURGESS [*not daring to believe such good news*] No!

CANDIDA: Yes. He had a seven day bill for £55 in his pocket when James found him on the Embankment. He thought he couldnt get any money for it until the seven days were up; and he was too shy to ask for credit. Oh, he's a dear boy! We are very fond of him.

BURGESS [*pretending to belittle the aristocracy, but with his eyes gleaming*] Mm! I thort you wouldnt git a hearl's nevvy visitin in Victawriar Pawrk unless he were a bit of a flat. [*Looking again at the picture*] Of course I dont old with that picture, Candy; but still it's a 'igh class fust rate work of ort: I can see that. Be sure you hintrodooce me to im, Candy. [*He looks at his watch anxiously*]. I can ony stay about two minutes.

Morell comes back with Eugene, whom Burgess contemplates moist-eyed with enthusiasm. He is a strange, shy youth of eighteen, slight, effeminate, with a delicate childish voice, and a hunted tormented expression and shrinking manner that shew the painful sensitiveness of very swift and acute apprehensiveness in youth, before the character has grown to its full strength. Miserably irresolute, he does not know where to stand or what to do. He is afraid of Burgess, and would run away into solitude if he dared; but the very intensity with which he feels a perfectly commonplace position comes from excessive nervous force; and his nostrils, mouth, and eyes betray a fiercely petulant wilfulness, as to the bent of which his brow, already lined with pity, is reassuring. He is so uncommon as to be almost unearthly; and to prosaic people there is something noxious in this unearthliness, just as to poetic people there is something angelic in it. His dress is anarchic. He wears an old blue serge jacket, unbuttoned, over a woollen lawn tennis shirt, with a silk handkerchief for a cravat, trousers matching the jacket, and brown canvas shoes. In these garments he has apparently lain in the heather and waded through the waters; and there is no evidence of his having ever brushed them.

As he catches sight of a stranger on entering, he stops, and edges along the wall on the opposite side of the room.

MORELL [*as he enters*] Come along: you can spare us quarter of an hour at all events. This is my father-in-law. Mr Burgess—Mr Marchbanks.

MARCHBANKS [*nervously backing against the bookcase*] Glad to meet you, sir.

BURGESS [*crossing to him with great heartiness, whilst Morell joins Candida at the fire*] Glad to meet you, I'm shore, Mr Morchbanks. [*Forcing him to shake hands*] Ow do you find yoreself this weather? Ope you aint lettin James put no foolish ideas into your ed?

MARCHBANKS: Foolish ideas? Oh, you mean Socialism? No.

BURGESS: Thats right. [*Again looking at his watch*] Well, I must go now: theres no elp for it. Yore not comin my way, orr you, Mr Morchbanks?

MARCHBANKS: Which way is that?

BURGESS: Victawriar Pawrk Station. Theres a city train at 12.25.

MORELL: Nonsense. Eugene will stay to lunch with us, I expect.

MARCHBANKS [*anxiously excusing himself*] No—I—I—

BURGESS: Well, well, I shornt press you: I bet youd rather lunch with Candy. Some night, I ope, youll come and dine with me at my club, the Freeman Founders in Nortn Folgit. Come: say you will!

MARCHBANKS: Thank you, Mr Burgess. Where is Norton Folgate? Down in Surrey, isnt it?

Burgess, inexpressibly tickled, begins to splutter with laughter.

CANDIDA [*coming to the rescue*] Youll lose your train, papa, if you dont go at once. Come back in the afternoon and tell Mr Marchbanks where to find the club.

BURGESS [*roaring with glee*] Down in Surrey! Har, har! thats not a bad one. Well, I never met a man as didnt know Nortn Folgit afore. [*Abashed at his own noisiness*] Goodbye, Mr Morchbanks: I know youre too ighbred to take my pleasantry in bad part. [*He again offers his hand*].

MARCHBANKS [*taking it with a nervous jerk*] Not at all.

BURGESS: Bye, bye, Candy. I'll look in again later on. So long, James.

MORELL: Must you go?

BURGESS: Dont stir. [*He goes out with unabated heartiness*].

MORELL: Oh, I'll see you off. [*He follows him*].

Eugene stares after them apprehensively, holding his breath until Burgess disappears.

CANDIDA [*laughing*] Well, Eugene? [*He turns with a start, and comes eagerly towards her, but stops irresolutely as he meets her amused look*]. What do you think of my father?

MARCHBANKS: I—I hardly know him yet. He seems to be a very nice old gentleman.

CANDIDA [*with gentle irony*] And youll go to the Freeman Founders to dine with him, wont you?

MARCHBANKS [*miserably, taking it quite seriously*] Yes, if it will please you.

CANDIDA [*touched*] Do you know, you are a very nice boy Eugene, with all your queerness. If you had laughed at my father I shouldnt have minded; but I like you ever so much better for being nice to him.

MARCHBANKS: Ought I to have laughed? I noticed that he said something funny; but I am so ill at ease with strangers; and I never can see a joke. I'm very sorry. [*He sits down on the sofa, his elbows on his knees and his temples between his fists, with an expression of hopeless suffering*].

CANDIDA [*bustling him goodnaturedly*] Oh come! You great baby, you! You are worse than usual this morning. Why were you so melancholy as we came along in the cab?

MARCHBANKS: Oh, that was nothing. I was wondering how much I ought to give the cabman. I know it's utterly silly; but you dont know how dreadful such things are to me—how I shrink from having to deal with strange people [*Quickly and reassuringly*] But it's all right. He beamed all over and touched his hat when Morell gave him two shillings. I was on the point of offering him ten.

Morell comes back with a few letters and newspapers which have come by the midday post.

CANDIDA: Oh, James dear, he was going to give the cabman ten shillings! ten shillings for a three minutes drive! Oh dear!

MORELL [*at the table, glancing through the letters*] Never mind her, Marchbanks. The overpaying instinct is a generous one: better than the underpaying instinct, and not so common.

MARCHBANKS [*relapsing into dejection*] No: cowardice, incompetence. Mrs Morell's quite right.

CANDIDA: Of course she is. [*She takes up her handbag*]. And now I must leave you to James for the present. I suppose you are too much of a poet to know the state a woman finds her house in when she's been away for three weeks. Give me my rug. [*Eugene takes the strapped rug from the couch, and gives it to her. She takes it in her left hand, having the bag in her right*]. Now hang my cloak across my arm. [*He obeys*]. Now my hat. [*He puts it into the hand which has the bag*]. Now open the door for me. [*He hurries before her and opens the door*]. Thanks. [*She goes out; and Marchbanks shuts the door*].

MORELL [*still busy at the table*] Youll stay to lunch, Marchbanks, of course.

MARCHBANKS [*scared*] I mustnt. [*He glances quickly at Morell, but at once avoids his frank look, and adds, with obvious disingenuousness*] I mean I cant.

MORELL: You mean you wont.

MARCHBANKS [*earnestly*] No: I should like to, indeed. Thank you very much. But—but—

MORELL: But—but—but—but—Bosh! If youd like to stay, stay. If youre shy, go and take a turn in the park and write poetry until half past one; and then come in and have a good feed.

MARCHBANKS: Thank you, I should like that very much. But I really mustnt. The truth is, Mrs Morell told me not to. She said she didnt think youd ask me to stay to lunch, but that I was to remember, if you did, that you didnt really want me to. [*Plaintively*] She said I'd understand; but I dont. Please dont tell her I told you.

MORELL [*drolly*] Oh, is that all? Wont my suggestion that you should take a turn in the park meet the difficulty?

MARCHBANKS: How?

MORELL [*exploding good-humoredly*] Why, you duffer—[*But this boisterousness jars himself as well as Eugene. He checks himself*]. No: I wont put it in that way. [*He comes to Eugene with affectionate seriousness*]. My dear lad: in a happy marriage like ours, there is something very sacred in the return of the wife to her home. [*Marchbanks looks quickly at him, half anticipating his meaning*]. An old friend or a truly noble and sympathetic soul is not in the way on such occasions; but a chance visitor is. [*The hunted horror-stricken expression comes out with sudden vividness in Eugene's face as he understands. Morell, occupied with his own thoughts, goes on without noticing this*]. Candida thought I would rather not have you here; but she was wrong. I'm very fond of you, my boy; and I should like you to see for yourself what a happy thing it is to be married as I am.

MARCHBANKS: Happy! Your marriage! You think that! You believe that!

MORELL [*buoyantly*] I know it, my lad. Larochefoucauld said that there are convenient marriages but no delightful ones. You dont know the comfort of seeing through and through a thundering liar and rotten cynic like that fellow. Ha! ha! Now, off with you to the park, and write your poem. Half past one, sharp, mind: we never wait for anybody.

MARCHBANKS [*wildly*] No: stop: you shant. I'll force it into the light.

MORELL [*puzzled*] Eh? Force what?

MARCHBANKS: I must speak to you. There is something that must be settled between us.

MORELL [*with a whimsical glance at his watch*] Now?

MARCHBANKS [*passionately*] Now. Before you leave this room. [*He retreats a few steps, and stands as if to bar Morell's way to the door*].

MORELL [*without moving, and gravely, perceiving now that there is something serious the matter*] I'm not going to leave it my dear boy: I thought you were. [*Eugene, baffled by his firm tone, turns his back on him, writhing with anger.*

Morell goes to him and puts his hand on his shoulder strongly and kindly, disregarding his attempt to shake it off]. Come: sit down quietly; and tell me what it is. And remember: we are friends, and need not fear that either of us will be anything but patient and kind to the other, whatever we may have to say.

MARCHBANKS [*twisting himself round on him*] Oh, I am not forgetting myself: I am only [*covering his face desperately with his hands*] full of horror. [*Then, dropping his hands, and thrusting his face forward fiercely at Morell, he goes on threateningly*] You shall see whether this is a time for patience and kindness. [*Morell, firm as a rock, looks indulgently at him*]. Dont you look at me in that self-complacent way. You think yourself stronger than I am; but I shall stagger you if you have a heart in your breast.

MORELL [*powerfully confident*] Stagger me, my boy. Out with it.

MARCHBANKS: First—

MORELL: First?

MARCHBANKS: I love your wife.

Morell recoils, and, after staring at him for a moment in utter amazement, bursts into uncontrollable laughter. Eugene is taken aback, but not disconcerted; and he soon becomes indignant and contemptuous.

MORELL [*sitting down to have his laugh out*] Why, my dear child, of course you do. Everybody loves her: they cant help it. I like it. But [*looking up jocosely at him*] I say, Eugene: do you think yours is a case to be talked about? Youre under twenty: she's over thirty. Doesnt it look rather too like a case of calf love?

MARCHBANKS [*vehemently*] You dare say that of her! You think that way of the love she inspires! It is an insult to her!

MORELL [*rising quickly, in an altered tone*] To her! Eugene: take care. I have been patient. I hope to remain patient. But there are some things I wont allow. Dont force me to shew you the indulgence I should shew to a child. Be a man.

MARCHBANKS [*with a gesture as if sweeping something behind him*] Oh, let us put aside all that cant. It horrifies me when I think of the doses of it she has had to endure in all the weary

years during which you have selfishly and blindly sacrificed
her to minister to your self-sufficiency: you! [*turning on him*]
who have not one thought—one sense—in common with
her.

MORELL [*philosophically*] She seems to bear it pretty well.
[*Looking at him straight in the face*] Eugene, my boy: you
are making a fool of yourself: a very great fool of yourself.
Theres a piece of wholesome plain speaking for you. [*He
knocks in the lesson with a nod in his old way, and posts
himself on the hearthrug, holding his hands behind him to
warm them*].

MARCHBANKS: Oh, do you think I dont know all that? Do you
think that the things people make fools of themselves about
are any less real and true than the things they behave sensi-
bly about? [*Morell's gaze wavers for the first time. He forgets to warm his hands, and stands listening, startled and
thoughtful*]. They are more true: they are the only things that
are true. You are very calm and sensible and moderate with
me because you can see that I am a fool about your wife; just
as no doubt that old man who was here just now is very wise
over your Socialism, because he sees that you are a fool
about it. [*Morell's perplexity deepens markedly. Eugene
follows up his advantage, plying him fiercely with questions*]. Does that prove you wrong? Does your complacent
superiority to me prove that I am wrong?

MORELL: Marchbanks: some devil is putting these words into
your mouth. It is easy—terribly easy—to shake a man's faith
in himself. To take advantage of that to break a man's spirit is
devil's work. Take care of what you are doing. Take care.

MARCHBANKS [*ruthlessly*] I know. I'm doing it on purpose. I
told you I should stagger you.

*They confront one another threateningly for a moment.
Then Morell recovers his dignity.*

MORELL [*with noble tenderness*] Eugene: listen to me. Some
day, I hope and trust, you will be a happy man like me. [*Eugene chafes intolerantly, repudiating the worth of his happiness. Morell, deeply insulted, controls himself with fine
forebearance, and continues steadily with great artistic*

beauty of delivery] You will be married; and you will be working with all your might and valor to make every spot on earth as happy as your own home. You will be one of the makers of the Kingdom of Heaven on earth; and—who knows?—you may be a master builder where I am only a humble journeyman; for dont think, my boy, that I cannot see in you, young as you are, promise of higher powers than I can ever pretend to. I well know that it is in the poet that the holy spirit of man—the god within him—is most godlike. It should make you tremble to think of that—to think that the heavy burthen and great gift of a poet may be laid upon you.

MARCHBANKS [*unimpressed and remorseless, his boyish crudity of assertion telling sharply against Morell's oratory*] It does not make me tremble. It is the want of it in others that makes me tremble.

MORELL [*redoubling his force of style under the stimulus of his genuine feeling and Eugene's obduracy*] Then help to kindle it in them—in me—not to extinguish it. In the future, when you are as happy as I am, I will be your true brother in the faith. I will help you to believe that God has given us a world that nothing but our own folly keeps from being a paradise. I will help you to believe that every stroke of your work is sowing happiness for the great harvest that all—even the humblest—shall one day reap. And last, but trust me, not least, I will help you to believe that your wife loves you and is happy in her home. We need such help, Marchbanks: we need it greatly and always. There are so many things to make us doubt, if once we let our understanding be troubled. Even at home, we sit as if in camp, encompassed by a hostile army of doubts. Will you play the traitor and let them in on me?

MARCHBANKS [*looking round wildly*] Is it like this for her here always? A woman, with a great soul, craving for reality, truth, freedom; and being fed on metaphors, sermons, stale perorations, mere rhetoric. Do you think a woman's soul can live on your talent for preaching?

MORELL [*stung*] Marchbanks: you make it hard for me to control myself. My talent is like yours insofar as it has any real worth at all. It is the gift of finding words for divine truth.

MARCHBANKS [*impetuously*] It's the gift of the gab, nothing more and nothing less. What has your knack of fine talking to do with the truth, any more than playing the organ has? Ive never been in your church; but Ive been to your political meetings; and Ive seen you do whats called rousing the meeting to enthusiasm: that is, you excited them until they behaved exactly as if they were drunk. And their wives looked on and saw what fools they were. Oh, it's an old story: youll find it in the Bible. I imagine King David, in his fits of enthusiasm, was very like you. [*Stabbing him with the words*] "But his wife despised him in her heart."

MORELL [*wrathfully*] Leave my house. Do you hear? [*He advances on him threateningly*].

MARCHBANKS [*shrinking back against the couch*] Let me alone. Dont touch me. [*Morell grasps him powerfully by the lappell of his coat: he cowers down on the sofa and screams passionately*] Stop, Morell: if you strike me, I'll kill myself: I wont bear it. [*Almost in hysterics*] Let me go. Take your hand away.

MORELL [*with slow emphatic scorn*] You little snivelling cowardly whelp. [*He releases him*]. Go, before you frighten yourself into a fit.

MARCHBANKS [*on the sofa, gasping, but relieved by the withdrawal of Morell's hand*] I'm not afraid of you: it's you who are afraid of me.

MORELL [*quietly, as he stands over him*] It looks like it doesnt it?

MARCHBANKS [*with petulant vehemence*] Yes, it does. [*Morell turns away contemptuously. Eugene scrambles to his feet and follows him*]. You think because I shrink from being brutally handled—because [*with tears in his voice*] I can do nothing but cry with rage when I am met with violence—because I cant lift a heavy trunk down from the top of a cab like you—because I cant fight you for your wife as a drunken navvy would: all that makes you think I'm afraid of you. But youre wrong. If I havnt got what you call British pluck, I havnt British cowardice either: I'm not afraid of a clergyman's ideas. I'll fight your ideas. I'll rescue her from slavery to them. I'll pit my own ideas against them. You are driving me out of the house because you darent let her choose between your ideas and mine. You are afraid to let me see her again. [*Morell, angered, turns suddenly on him. He flies to the door in involuntary dread*]. Let me alone, I say. I'm going.

MORELL [*with cold scorn*] Wait a moment: I am not going to touch you: dont be afraid. When my wife comes back she will want to know why you have gone. And when she finds that you are never going to cross our threshold again, she will want to have that explained too. Now I dont wish to distress her by telling her that you have behaved like a blackguard.

MARCHBANKS [*coming back with renewed vehemence*] You shall. You must. If you give any explanation but the true one, you are a liar and a coward. Tell her what I said; and how you were strong and manly, and shook me as a terrier shakes a rat; and how I shrank and was terrified; and how you called me a snivelling little whelp and put me out of the house. If you dont tell her, I will: I'll write it to her.

MORELL [*puzzled*] Why do you want her to know this?

MARCHBANKS [*with lyric rapture*] Because she will understand me, and know that I understand her. If you keep back one word of it from her—if you are not ready to lay the truth at her feet as I am—then you will know to the end of your days that she really belongs to me and not to you. Goodbye. [*Going*].

MORELL [*terribly disquieted*] Stop: I will not tell her.

MARCHBANKS [*turning near the door*] Either the truth or a lie you must tell her, if I go.

MORELL [*temporizing*] Marchbanks: it is sometimes justifiable—

MARCHBANKS [*cutting him short*] I know: to lie. It will be useless. Goodbye, Mr Clergyman.

As he turns to the door, it opens and Candida enters in her housekeeping dress.

CANDIDA: Are you going, Eugene? [*Looking more observantly at him*] Well, dear me, just look at you, going out into the street in that state! You are a poet, certainly. Look at him,

James! [*She takes him by the coat, and brings him forward, shewing him to Morell*]. Look at his collar! look at his tie! look at his hair! One would think somebody had been throttling you. [*Eugene instinctively rises to look round at Morell; but she pulls him back*]. Here! Stand still. [*She buttons his collar; ties his neckerchief in a bow; and arranges his hair*]. There! Now you look so nice that I think youd better stay to lunch after all, though I told you you mustnt. It will be ready in half an hour. [*She puts a final touch to the bow. He kisses her hand*]. Dont be silly.

MARCHBANKS: I want to stay, of course; unless the reverend gentleman your husband has anything to advance to the contrary.

CANDIDA: Shall he stay, James, if he promises to be a good boy and help me to lay the table?

MORELL [*shortly*] Oh yes, certainly: he had better. [*He goes to the table and pretends to busy himself with his papers there*].

MARCHBANKS [*offering his arm to Candida*] Come and lay the table. [*She takes it. They go to the door together. As they pass out he adds*] I am the happiest of mortals.

MORELL: So was I—an hour ago.

ACT II

The same day later in the afternoon. The same room. The chair for visitors has been replaced at the table. Marchbanks, alone and idle, is trying to find out how the typewriter works. Hearing someone at the door, he steals guiltily away to the window and pretends to be absorbed in the view. Miss Garnett, carrying the notebook in which she takes down Morell's letters in shorthand from his dictation, sits down at the typewriter and sets to work transcribing them, much too busy to notice Eugene. When she begins the second line she stops and stares at the machine. Something wrong evidently.

PROSERPINE: Bother! Youve been meddling with my type-writer, Mr Marchbanks; and theres not the least use in your trying to look as if you hadnt.

MARCHBANKS [*timidly*] I'm very sorry, Miss Garnett. I only tried to make it write. [*Plaintively*] But it wouldnt.

PROSERPINE: Well, youve altered the spacing.

MARCHBANKS [*earnestly*] I assure you I didnt. I didnt indeed. I only turned a little wheel. It gave a sort of click.

PROSERPINE: Oh, now I understand. [*She restores the spacing, talking volubly all the time*] I suppose you thought it was a sort of barrel-organ. Nothing to do but turn the handle, and it would write a beautiful love letter for you straight off, eh?

MARCHBANKS [*seriously*] I suppose a machine could be made to write love letters. Theyre all the same, arnt they?

PROSERPINE [*somewhat indignantly: any such discussion, except by way of pleasantry, being outside her code of manners*] How do I know? Why do you ask me?

MARCHBANKS: I beg your pardon. I thought clever people—people who can do business and write letters and that sort of thing—always had to have love affairs to keep them from going mad.

PROSERPINE [*rising, outraged*] Mr Marchbanks! [*She looks severely at him, and marches majestically to the bookcase*].

MARCHBANKS [*approaching her humbly*] I hope I havnt offended you. Perhaps I shouldnt have alluded to your love affairs.

PROSERPINE [*plucking a blue book from the shelf and turning sharply on him*] I havnt any love affairs. How dare you say such a thing? The idea! [*She tucks the book under her arm, and is flouncing back to her machine when he addresses her with awakened interest and sympathy*].

MARCHBANKS: Really! Oh, then you are shy, like me.

PROSERPINE: Certainly I am not shy. What do you mean?

MARCHBANKS [*secretly*] You must be: that is the reason there are so few love affairs in the world. We all go about longing for love: it is the first need of our natures, the first prayer of our hearts; but we dare not utter our longing: we are too shy. [*Very earnestly*] Oh, Miss Garnett, what would you not give to be without fear, without shame—

PROSERPINE [*scandalized*] Well, upon my word!

MARCHBANKS [*with petulant impatience*] Ah, dont say those stupid things to me: they dont deceive me: what use are they? Why are you afraid to be your real self with me? I am just like you.

PROSERPINE: Like me! Pray are you flattering me or flattering yourself? I dont feel quite sure which. [*She again tries to get back to her work*].

MARCHBANKS [*stopping her mysteriously*] Hush! I go about in search of love; and I find it in unmeasured stores in the bosoms of others. But when I try to ask for it, this horrible shyness strangles me; and I stand dumb, or worse than dumb, saying meaningless things: foolish lies. And I see the affection I am longing for given to dogs and cats and pet birds, because they come and ask for it. [*Almost whispering*] It must be asked for: it is like a ghost: it cannot speak unless it is first spoken to. [*At his usual pitch, but with deep melancholy*] All the love in the world is longing to speak; only it dare not, because it is shy! shy! shy! That is the world's tragedy. [*With a deep sigh he sits in the visitors' chair and buries his face in his hands*].

PROSERPINE [*amazed, but keeping her wits about her: her point of honor in encounters with strange young men*] Wicked people get over that shyness occasionally, dont they?

MARCHBANKS [*scrambling up almost fiercely*] Wicked people means people who have no love: therefore they have no shame. They have the power to ask love because they dont need it: they have the power to offer it because they have none to give. [*He collapses into his seat, and adds, mournfully*] But we, who have love, and long to mingle it with the love of others: we cannot utter a word. [*Timidly*] You find that, dont you?

PROSERPINE: Look here: if you dont stop talking like this, I'll leave the room, Mr. Marchbanks: I really will. It's not proper.

She resumes her seat at the typewriter, opening the blue book and preparing to copy a passage from it.

MARCHBANKS [*hopelessly*] Nothing thats worth saying is proper. [*He rises, and wanders about the room in his lost way*]. I cant understand you, Miss Garnett. What am I to talk about?

PROSERPINE [*snubbing him*] Talk about indifferent things. Talk about the weather.

MARCHBANKS: Would you talk about indifferent things if a child were by, crying bitterly with hunger?

PROSERPINE: I suppose not.

MARCHBANKS: Well: *I* cant talk about indifferent things with my heart crying out bitterly in its hunger.

PROSERPINE: Then hold your tongue.

MARCHBANKS: Yes: that is what it always comes to. We hold our tongues. Does that stop the cry of your heart? for it does cry: doesnt it? It must, if you have a heart.

PROSERPINE [*suddenly rising with her hand pressed on her heart*] Oh, it's no use trying to work while you talk like that.

[*She leaves her little table and sits on the sofa. Her feelings are keenly stirred*]. It's no business of yours whether my heart cries or not; but I have a mind to tell you, for all that.

MARCHBANKS: You neednt. I know already that it must.

PROSERPINE: But mind! if you ever say I said so, I'll deny it.

MARCHBANKS [*compassionately*] Yes, I know. And so you havnt the courage to tell him?

PROSERPINE [*bouncing up*] Him! Who?

MARCHBANKS: Whoever he is. The man you love. It might be anybody. The curate, Mr Mill, perhaps.

PROSERPINE [*with disdain*] Mr Mill!!! A fine man to break my heart about, indeed! I'd rather have you than Mr Mill.

MARCHBANKS [*recoiling*] No, really: I'm very sorry; but you mustnt think of that. I—

PROSERPINE [*testily, going to the fireplace and standing at it with her back to him*] Oh, dont be frightened: it's not you. It's not any one particular person.

MARCHBANKS: I know. You feel that you could love anybody that offered—

PROSERPINE [*turning, exasperated*] Anybody that offered! No, I do not. What do you take me for?

MARCHBANKS [*discouraged*] No use. You wont make me real answers: only those things that everybody says. [*He strays to the sofa and sits down disconsolately*].

PROSERPINE [*nettled at what she takes to be a disparagement of her manners by an aristocrat*] Oh well, if you want original conversation, youd better go and talk to yourself.

MARCHBANKS: That is what all poets do: they talk to themselves out loud; and the world overhears them. But it's horrible lonely not to hear someone else talk sometimes.

PROSERPINE: Wait until Mr Morell comes. He'll talk to you. [*Marchbanks shudders*]. Oh, you neednt make wry faces over him: he can talk better than you. [*With temper*] He'd talk your little head off. [*She is going back angrily to her place, when he, suddenly enlightened, springs up and stops her*].

MARCHBANKS: Ah! I understand now.

PROSERPINE [*reddening*] What do you understand?

MARCHBANKS: Your secret. Tell me: is it really and truly possible for a woman to love him?

PROSERPINE [*as if this were beyond all bounds*] Well!!

MARCHBANKS [*passionately*] No: answer me. I want to know: I must know. *I* cant understand it. I can see nothing in him but words, pious resolutions, what people call goodness. You cant love that.

PROSERPINE [*attempting to snub him by an air of cool propriety*] I simply dont know what youre talking about. I dont understand you.

MARCHBANKS [*vehemently*] You do. You lie.

PROSERPINE: Oh!

MARCHBANKS: You do understand; and you know. [*Determined to have an answer*] Is it possible for a woman to love him?

PROSERPINE [*looking him straight in the face*] Yes. [*He covers his face with his hands*]. Whatever is the matter with you! [*He takes down his hands. Frightened at the tragic mask presented to her, she hurries past him at the utmost possible distance, keeping her eyes on his face until he turns from her and goes to the child's chair beside the hearth, where he sits in the deepest dejection. As she approaches the door, it opens and Burgess enters. Seeing him, she ejaculates*] Praise heaven! here's somebody [*and feels safe enough to resume her place at her table. She puts a fresh sheet of paper into the typewriter as Burgess crosses to Eugene*].

BURGESS [*bent on taking care of the distinguished visitor*] Well: so this is the way they leave you to yoreself, Mr Morchbanks. Ive come to keep you company. [*Marchbanks looks up at him in consternation, which is quite lost on him*]. James is receivin a deppitation in the dinin room; and Candy is hupstairs heducating of a young stitcher gurl she's hinterested in. [*Condolingly*] You must find it lonesome here with no one but the typist to talk to. [*He pulls round the easy chair, and sits down*].

PROSERPINE [*highly incensed*] He'll be all right now that he has the advantage of your polished conversation: thats one comfort, anyhow. [*She begins to typewrite with clattering asperity*].

BURGESS [*amazed at her audacity*] Hi was not addressin myself to you, young woman, that I'm awerr of.

PROSERPINE: Did you ever see worse manners, Mr Marchbanks?

BURGESS [*with pompous severity*] Mr Morchbanks is a gentleman, and knows his place, which is more than some people do.

PROSERPINE [*fretfully*] It's well you and I are not ladies and gentlemen: I'd talk to you pretty straight if Mr Marchbanks wasnt here. [*She pulls the letter out of the machine so crossly that it tears*]. There! now I've spoiled this letter! have to be done all over again! Oh, I cant contain myself: silly old fathead!

BURGESS [*rising, breathless with indignation*] Ho! I'm a silly ole fat'ead, am I? Ho, indeed [*gasping*]! Hall right, my gurl! Hall right. You just wait till I tell that to yore hemployer. Youll see. I'll teach you: see if I don't.

PROSERPINE [*conscious of having gone too far*] I—

BURGESS [*cutting her short*] Ho: youve done it now. No huse a-talkin to me. I'll let you know who I am. [*Proserpine shifts her paper carriage with a defiant bang, and disdainfully goes on with her work*]. Dont you take no notice of her, Mr Morchbanks. She's beneath it. [*He loftily sits down again*].

MARCHBANKS [*miserably nervous and disconcerted*] Hadnt we better change the subject? I—I dont think Miss Garnett meant anything.

PROSERPINE [*with intense conviction*] Oh, didnt I though, just!

BURGESS: I wouldn't demean myself to take notice on her.

An electric bell rings twice.

PROSERPINE [*gathering up her notebook and papers*] Thats for me. [*She hurries out*].

BURGESS [*calling after her*]. Oh, we can spare you. [*Somewhat relieved by the triumph of having the last word, and yet half inclined to try to improve on it, he looks after her for a moment; then subsides into his seat by Eugene, and addresses him very confidentially*]. Now we're alone, Mr Morchbanks, let me give you a friendly int that I wouldnt give to heverybody. Ow long ave you known my son-in-law James ere?

MARCHBANKS: I dont know. I never can remember dates. A few months, perhaps.

BURGESS: Ever notice hennythink queer about him?

MARCHBANKS: I dont think so.

BURGESS [*impressively*] No more you wouldnt. Thats the danger on it. Well, he's mad.

MARCHBANKS: Mad!

BURGESS: Mad as a Morch 'are. You take notice on him and youll see.

MARCHBANKS [*uneasily*] But surely that is only because his opinions—

BURGESS [*touching him on the knee with his forefinger, and pressing it to hold his attention*] Thats the same what I hused to think, Mr Morchbanks. Hi thought long enough that it was ony his opinions; though, mind you, hopinions becomes vurry serious things when people takes to hactin on em as e does. But thats not what I go on. [*He looks round to make sure that they are alone, and bends over to Eugene's ear*]. What do you think he sez to me this mornin in this very room?

MARCHBANKS: What?

BURGESS: He sez to me—this is as sure as we're settin here now—he sez "I'm a fool," he sez; "and yore a scounderl." Me a scounderl, mind you! And then shook ands with me on it, as if it was to my credit! Do you mean to tell me as that man's sane?

MORELL [*outside, calling to Proserpine as he opens the door*] Get all their names and addresses, Miss Garnett.

PROSERPINE [*in the distance*] Yes, Mr Morell.

Morell comes in, with the deputation's documents in his hands.

BURGESS [*aside to Marchbanks*] Yorr he is. Just you keep your heye on im and see. [*Rising momentously*] I'm sorry, James, to ave to make a complaint to you. I dont want to do it; but I feel I oughter, as a matter o right and dooty.

MORELL: Whats the matter?

BURGESS: Mr Morchbanks will bear me hout: he was a wit-

ness. [*Very solemnly*] Yore young woman so far forgot herself as to call me a silly ole fat'ead.

MORELL [*with tremendous heartiness*] Oh, now, isnt that exactly like Prossy? She's so frank: she cant contain herself!
Poor Prossy! Ha! ha!

BURGESS [*trembling with rage*] And do you hexpec me to put
up with it from the like of er?

MORELL: Pooh, nonsense! you cant take any notice of it.
Never mind. [*He goes to the cellaret and puts the papers into
one of the drawers*].

BURGESS: Oh, Hi dont mind. Hi'm above it. But is it right?
thats what I want to know. Is it right?

MORELL: Thats a question for the Church, not for the laity.
Has it done you any harm? thats the question for you, eh? Of
course it hasnt. Think no more of it. [*He dismisses the subject by going to his place at the table and setting to work at
his correspondence*].

BURGESS [*aside to Marchbanks*] What did I tell you? Mad as a
atter. [*He goes to the table and asks, with the sickly civility
of a hungry man*] When's dinner, James?

MORELL: Not for a couple of hours yet.

BURGESS [*with plaintive resignation*] Gimme a nice book to
read over the fire, will you, James: thur's a good chap.

MORELL: What sort of book? A good one?

BURGESS [*with almost a yell of remonstrance*] Nah-oo! Sum-
mat pleasant, just to pass the time. [*Morell takes an illustrated paper from the table and offers it. He accepts it
humbly*]. Thank yer, James. [*He goes back to the big chair at
the fire, and sits there at his ease, reading*].

MORELL [*as he writes*] Candida will come to entertain you
presently. She has got rid of her pupil. She is filling the lamps.

MARCHBANKS [*starting up in the wildest consternation*] But
that will soil her hands. I cant bear that, Morell: it's a shame.
I'll go and fill them. [*He makes for the door*].

MORELL: Youd better not. [*Marchbanks stops irresolutely*].
She'd only set you to clean my boots, to save me the trouble
of doing it myself in the morning.

BURGESS [*with grave disapproval*] Dont you keep a servant now, James?

MORELL: Yes: but she isnt a slave; and the house looks as if I kept three. That means that everyone has to lend a hand. It's not a bad plan: Prossy and I can talk business after breakfast while we're washing up. Washing up's no trouble when there are two people to do it.

MARCHBANKS [*tormentedly*] Do you think every woman is as coarse-grained as Miss Garnett?

BURGESS [*emphatically*] Thats quite right, Mr Morchbanks: thats quite right. She is corse-grained.

MORELL [*quietly and significantly*] Marchbanks!

MARCHBANKS: Yes?

MORELL: How many servants does your father keep?

MARCHBANKS [*pettishly*] Oh, I dont know. [*He moves to the sofa, as if to get as far as possible from Morell's questioning, and sits down in great agony of spirit, thinking of the paraffin*].

MORELL [*very gravely*] So many that you dont know! [*More aggressively*] When theres anything coarse-grained to be done, you just ring the bell and throw it on to somebody else, eh?

MARCHBANKS: Oh, dont torture me. You dont even ring the bell. But your wife's beautiful fingers are dabbling in paraffin oil while you sit here comfortably preaching about it: ever-lasting preaching! preaching! words! words! words!

BURGESS [*intensely appreciating this retort*] Har, har! Devil a better! [*Radiantly*] Ad you there, James, straight.

   Candida comes in, well aproned, with a reading lamp trimmed, filled, and ready for lighting. She places it on the table near Morell, ready for use.

CANDIDA [*brushing her finger tips together with a slight twitch of her nose*] If you stay with us, Eugene, I think I will hand over the lamps to you.

MARCHBANKS: I will stay on condition that you hand over all the rough work to me.

CANDIDA: Thats very gallant; but I think I should like to see how you do it first. [*Turning to Morell*] James: youve not been looking after the house properly.

MORELL: What have I done—or not done—my love?

CANDIDA [*with serious vexation*] My own particular pet scrubbing brush has been used for blackleading. [*A heartbreaking wail bursts from Marchbanks. Burgess looks round, amazed. Candida hurries to the sofa*]. Whats the matter? Are you ill, Eugene?

MARCHBANKS: No: not ill. Only horror! horror! horror! [*He bows his head on his hands*].

BURGESS [*shocked*] What! Got the orrors, Mr Morchbanks! Oh, thats bad, at your age. You must leave it off grajally.

CANDIDA [*reassured*] Nonesense, papa! It's only poetic horror, isn't it, Eugene [*petting him*]?

BURGESS [*abashed*] Oh, poetic orror, is it? I beg your pordon, I'm shore. [*He turns to the fire again, deprecating his hasty conclusion*].

CANDIDA: What is it, Eugene? the scrubbing brush? [*He shudders*] Well, there! never mind. [*She sits down beside him*]. Wouldnt you like to present me with a nice new one, with an ivory back inlaid with mother-of-pearl?

MARCHBANKS [*softly and musically, but sadly and longingly*] No, not a scrubbing brush, but a boat: a tiny shallop to sail away in, far from the world, where the marble floors are washed by the rain and dried by the sun; where the south wind dusts the beautiful green and purple carpets. Or a chariot! to carry us up into the sky, where the lamps are stars, and dont need to be filled with paraffin oil every day.

MORELL [*harshly*] And where there is nothing to do but to be idle, selfish, and useless.

CANDIDA [*jarred*] Oh James! how could you spoil it all?

MARCHBANKS [*firing up*] Yes, to be idle, selfish, and useless: that is, to be beautiful and free and happy: hasnt every man desired that with all his soul for the woman he loves? Thats my ideal: what yours, and that of all the dreadful people who live in these hideous rows of houses? Sermons and scrubbing brushes! With you to preach the sermon and your wife to scrub.

CANDIDA [*quaintly*] He cleans the boots, Eugene. You will have to clean them to-morrow for saying that about him.

MARCHBANKS: Oh, dont talk about boots! Your feet should be beautiful on the mountains.

CANDIDA: My feet would not be beautiful on the Hackney Road without boots.

BURGESS [*scandalized*] Come, Candy! dont be vulgar. Mr Morchbanks aint accustomed to it. Youre givin him the orrors again. I mean the poetic ones.

> *Morell is silent. Apparently he is busy with his letters: really he is puzzling with misgiving over his new and alarming experience that the surer he is of his moral thrusts, the more swiftly and effectively Eugene parries them. To find himself beginning to fear a man whom he does not respect afflicts him bitterly.*
>
> *Miss Garnett comes in with a telegram.*

PROSERPINE [*handing the telegram to Morell*] Reply paid. The boy's waiting. [*To Candida, coming back to her machine and sitting down*] Maria is ready for you now in the kitchen, Mrs Morell [*Candida rises*]. The onions have come.

MARCHBANKS [*convulsively*] Onions!

CANDIDA: Yes, onions. Not even Spanish ones: nasty little red onions. You shall help me to slice them. Come along.

> *She catches him by the wrist and runs out, pulling him after her. Burgess rises in consternation, and stands aghast on the hearth-rug, staring after them.*

BURGESS: Candy didnt oughter andle a hearl's nevvy like that. It's goin too fur with it. Lookee ere, James: do e often git taken queer like that?

MORELL [*shortly, writing a telegram*] I dont know.

BURGESS [*sentimentally*] He talks very pretty. I awlus had a turn for a bit of poetry. Candy takes arter me that-a-way. Huseter make me tell er fairy stories when she was only a little kiddy not that igh [*indicating a stature of two feet or thereabouts*].

MORELL [*preoccupied*] Ah, indeed. [*He blots the telegram and goes out*].

PROSERPINE: Used you to make the fairy stories up out of your own head?

Burgess, not deigning to reply, strikes an attitude of the haughtiest disdain on the hearth-rug.

PROSERPINE [*calmly*] I should never have supposed you had it in you. By the way, I'd better warn you, since youve taken such a fancy to Mr Marchbanks. He's mad.

BURGESS: Mad! What! Im too!!

PROSERPINE: Mad as a March hare. He did frighten me, I can tell you, just before you came in that time. Havent you noticed the queer things he says?

BURGESS: So thats what the poetic orrors means. Blame me if it didnt come into my ed once or twyst that he was a bit horff is chump! [*He crosses the room to the door, lifting up his voice as he goes*]. Well, this is a pretty sort of asylum for a man to be in, with no one but you to take care of him!

PROSERPINE [*as he passes her*] Yes, what a dreadful thing it would be if anything happened to you!

BURGESS [*loftily*] Dont you haddress no remarks to me. Tell your hemployer that Ive gone into the gorden for a smoke.

PROSERPINE [*mocking*] Oh!

Before Burgess can retort, Morell comes back.

BURGESS [*sentimentally*] Going for a turn in the gording to smoke, James.

MORELL [*brusquely*] Oh, all right, all right. [*Burgess goes out pathetically in the character of a weary old man. Morell stands at the table, turning over his papers, and adding, across to Proserpine, half humorously, half absently*] Well, Miss Prossy, why have you been calling my father-in-law names?

PROSERPINE [*blushing fiery red, and looking quickly up at him, half scared, half reproachful*] I— [*She bursts into tears*].

MORELL [*with tender gaiety, leaning across the table towards her, and consoling her*] Oh, come! come! come! Never mind, Pross: he is a silly old fathead, isn't he?

With an explosive sob, she makes a dash at the door, and vanishes, banging it. Morell, shaking his head resignedly, sighs and goes wearily to his chair, where he sits down and sets to work, looking old and careworn.

Candida comes in. She has finished her household work and taken off the apron. She at once notices his dejected ap-

*pearance and posts herself quietly at the visitors' chair, look-
ing down at him attentively. She says nothing.*

MORELL [*looking up, but with his pen raised ready to resume
his work*] Well? Where is Eugene?

CANDIDA: Washing his hands in the scullery under the tap. He
will make an excellent cook if he can only get over his dread
of Maria.

MORELL [*shortly*] Ha! No doubt. [*He begins writing again*]

CANDIDA [*going nearer, and putting her hand down softly on
his to stop him as she says*] Come here, dear. Let me look at
you. [*He drops his pen and yields himself to her disposal. She
makes him rise, and brings him a little away from the table,
looking at him critically all the time*]. Turn your face to the
light. [*She places him facing the window*]. My boy is not
looking well. Has he been overworking?

MORELL: Nothing more than usual.

CANDIDA: He looks very pale, and grey, and wrinkled, and
old. [*His melancholy deepens: and she attacks it with wilful
gaiety*] Here: [*pulling him towards the easy chair*] youve done
enough writing for today. Leave Prossy to finish it. Come
and talk to me.

MORELL: But—

CANDIDA [*insisting*] Yes, I must be talked to. [*She makes him
sit down, and seats herself on the carpet beside his knee*].
Now [*patting his hand*] youre beginning to look better already. Why must you go out every night lecturing and talking? I hardly have one evening a week with you. Of course
what you say is all very true; but it does no good: they dont
mind what you say to them one little bit. They think they
agree with you; but whats the use of their agreeing with you
if they go and do just the opposite of what you tell them the
moment your back is turned? Look at our congregation at St
Dominic's! Why do they come to hear you talking about
Christianity every Sunday? Why, just because theyve been so
full of business and money-making for six days that they
want to forget all about it and have a rest on the seventh; so
that they can go back fresh and make money harder than
ever! You positively help them at it instead of hindering them.

MORELL [*with energetic seriousness*] You know very well Candida, that I often blow them up soundly for that. And if there is nothing in their churchgoing but rest and diversion, why dont they try something more amusing? more self-indulgent? There must be some good in the fact that they prefer St Dominic's to worse places on Sundays.

CANDIDA: Oh, the worse places arnt open; and even if they were, they darent be seen going to them. Besides, James dear, you preach so splendidly that it's as good as a play for them. Why do you think the women are so enthusiastic?

MORELL [*shocked*] Candida!

CANDIDA: Oh, *I* know. You silly boy: you think it's your Socialism and your religion; but if it were that, theyd do what you tell them instead of only coming to look at you. They all have Prossy's complaint.

MORELL: Prossy's complaint! What do you mean, Candida?

CANDIDA: Yes, Prossy, and all the other secretaries you ever had. Why does Prossy condescend to wash up the things, and to peel potatoes and abase herself in all manner of ways for six shillings a week less than she used to get in a city office? She's in love with you, James: thats the reason. Theyre all in love with you. And you are in love with preaching because you do it so beautifully. And you think it's all enthusiasm for the kingdom of Heaven on earth; and so do they. You dear silly!

MORELL: Candida: what dreadful! what soul-destroying cynicism! Are you jesting? Or—can it be?—are you jealous?

CANDIDA [*with curious thoughtfulness*] Yes, I feel a little jealous sometimes.

MORELL [*incredulously*] Of Prossy?

CANDIDA [*laughing*] No, no, no, no. Not jealous of anybody. Jealous for somebody else, who is not loved as he ought to be.

MORELL: Me?

CANDIDA: You! Why, youre spoiled with love and worship: you get far more than is good for you. No: I mean Eugene.

MORELL [*startled*] Eugene!

CANDIDA: It seems unfair that all the love should go to you, and none to him; although he needs it so much more than you do. [*A convulsive movement shakes him in spite of himself*]. Whats the matter? Am I worrying you?

MORELL [*hastily*] Not at all. [*Looking at her with troubled intensity*] You know that I have perfect confidence in you, Candida.

CANDIDA: You vain thing! Are you so sure of your irresistible attractions?

MORELL: Candida: you are shocking me. I never thought of my attractions. I thought of your goodness, of your purity. That is what I confide in.

CANDIDA: What a nasty uncomfortable thing to say to me! Oh, you are a clergyman, James: a thorough clergyman!

MORELL [*turning away from her, heart-stricken*] So Eugene says.

CANDIDA [*with lively interest, leaning over to him with her arms on his knee*] Eugene's always right. He's a wonderful boy: I have grown fonder and fonder of him all the time I was away. Do you know, James, that though he has not the least suspicion of it himself, he is ready to fall madly in love with me?

MORELL [*grimly*] Oh, he has no suspicion of it himself, hasnt he?

CANDIDA: Not a bit. [*She takes her arms from his knee, and turns thoughtfully, sinking into a more restful attitude with her hands in her lap*]. Some day he will know: when he is grown up and experienced, like you. And he will know that I must have known. I wonder what he will think of me then.

MORELL: No evil, Candida. I hope and trust, no evil.

CANDIDA [*dubiously*] That will depend.

MORELL [*bewildered*] Depend!

CANDIDA [*looking at him*] Yes: it will depend on what happens to him. [*He looks vacantly at her*]. Dont you see? It will depend on how he comes to learn what love really is. I mean on the sort of woman who will teach it to him.

MORELL [*quite at a loss*] Yes. No. I don't know what you mean.

CANDIDA [*explaining*] If he learns it from a good woman, then it will be all right: he will forgive me.

MORELL: Forgive?

CANDIDA: But suppose he learns it from a bad woman, as so many men do, especially poetic men, who imagine all women are angels! Suppose he only discovers the value of love when he has thrown it away and degraded himself in his ignorance! Will he forgive me then, do you think?

MORELL: Forgive you for what?

CANDIDA [*realizing how stupid he is, and a little disappointed, though quite tenderly so*] Dont you understand? [*He shakes his head. She turns to him again, so as to explain with the fondest intimacy*]. I mean, will he forgive me for not teaching him myself? For abandoning him to the bad women for the sake of my goodness, of my purity, as you call it? Ah, James, how little you understand me, to talk of your confidence in my goodness and purity! I would give them both to poor Eugene as willingly as I would give my shawl to a beggar dying of cold, if there were nothing else to restrain me. Put your trust in my love for you, James; for if that went, I should care very little for your sermons: mere phrases that you cheat yourself and others with every day. [*She is about to rise*].

MORELL: His words!

CANDIDA [*checking herself quickly in the act of getting up*] Whose words?

MORELL: Eugene's.

CANDIDA [*delighted*] He is always right. He understands you; he understands me; he understands Prossy; and you, darling, you understand nothing. [*She laughs, and kisses him to console him. He recoils as if stabbed, and springs up*].

MORELL: How can you bear to do that when— Oh, Candida [*with anguish in his voice*] I had rather you had plunged a grappling iron into my heart than given me that kiss.

CANDIDA [*amazed*] My dear: whats the matter?

MORELL [*frantically waving her off*] Dont touch me.

CANDIDA: James!!!

    They are interrupted by the entrance of Marchbanks with Burgess, who stop near the door, staring.

MARCHBANKS: Is anything the matter?

MORELL [*deadly white, putting an iron constraint on himself*]

Nothing but this: that either you were right this morning, or Candida is mad.

BURGESS [*in modest protest*] What! Candy mad too! Oh, come! come! come! [*He crosses the room to the fireplace, protesting as he goes, and knocks the ashes out of his pipe on the bars*].

Morell sits down at his table desperately, leaning forward to hide his face, and interlacing his fingers rigidly to keep them steady.

CANDIDA [*to Morell, relieved and laughing*] Oh, youre only shocked! Is that all? How conventional all you unconventional people are! [*She sits gaily on the arm of the chair*].

BURGESS: Come: be'ave yourself, Candy. Whatll Mr Morchbanks think of you?

CANDIDA: This comes of James teaching me to think for myself, and never to hold back out of fear of what other people may think of me. It works beautifully as long as I think the same things as he does. But now! because I have just thought something different! look at him! Just look! [*She points to Morell, greatly amused*].

Eugene looks, and instantly presses his hand on his heart, as if some pain had shot through it. He sits down on the sofa like a man witnessing a tragedy.

BURGESS [*on the hearthrug*] Well, James, you certnly haint as himpressive lookin as usu'l.

MORELL [*with a laugh which is half a sob*] I suppose not. I beg all your pardons: I was not conscious of making a fuss. [*Pulling himself together*] Well, well, well, well, well! [*He sets to work at his papers again with resolute cheerfulness*].

CANDIDA [*going to the sofa and sitting beside Marchbanks, still in a bantering humor*] Well, Eugene: why are you so sad? Did the onions make you cry?

MARCHBANKS [*aside to her*] It is your cruelty. I hate cruelty. It is a horrible thing to see one person make another suffer.

CANDIDA [*petting him ironically*] Poor boy! have I been cruel? Did I make it slice nasty little red onions?

MARCHBANKS [*earnestly*] Oh, stop, stop: I dont mean myself. You have made him suffer frightfully. I feel his pain in my own heart. I know that it is not your fault: it is something

that must happen; but don't make light of it. I shudder when
you torture him and laugh.

CANDIDA [*incredulously*] I torture James! Nonsense, Eugene:
how you exaggerate! Silly! [*She rises and goes to the table,
a little troubled*]. Dont work any more, dear. Come and talk
to us.

MORELL [*affectionately but bitterly*] Ah no: I cant talk. I can
only preach.

CANDIDA [*caressing his hand*] Well, come and preach.

BURGESS [*strongly remonstrating*] Aw no, Candy. Ang it all!

  Lexy Mill comes in, anxious and important.

LEXY [*hastening to shake hands with Candida*] How do you
do, Mrs Morell? So glad to see you back again.

CANDIDA: Thank you, Lexy. You know Eugene, dont you?

LEXY: Oh yes. How do you do, Marchbanks?

MARCHBANKS: Quite well, thanks.

LEXY [*to Morell*] Ive just come from the Guild of St
Matthew. They are in the greatest consternation about your
telegram.

CANDIDA: What did you telegraph about, James?

LEXY [*to Candida*] He was to have spoken for them tonight.
Theyve taken the large hall in Mare Street and spent a lot of
money on posters. Morell's telegram was to say he couldnt
come. It came on them like a thunderbolt.

CANDIDA [*surprised, and beginning to suspect something
wrong*] Given up an engagement to speak!

BURGESS: Fust time in his life, I'll bet. Aint it, Candy?

LEXY [*to Morell*] They decided to send an urgent telegram to
you asking whether you could not change your mind. Have
you received it?

MORELL [*with restrained impatience*] Yes, yes: I got it.

LEXY: It was reply paid.

MORELL: Yes, I know. I answered it. I cant go.

CANDIDA: But why, James?

MORELL [*almost fiercely*] Because I dont choose. These people
forget that I am a man: they think I am a talking machine to
be turned on for their pleasure every evening of my life. May
I not have one night at home, with my wife, and my friends?

They are all amazed at this outburst, except Eugene. His expression remains unchanged.

CANDIDA: Oh, James, you mustnt mind what I said about that. And if you dont go youll have an attack of bad conscience tomorrow.

LEXY [*intimidated, but urgent*] I know, of course, that they make the most unreasonable demands on you. But they have been telegraphing all over the place for another speaker; and they can get nobody but the President of the Agnostic League.

MORELL [*promptly*] Well, an excellent man. What better do they want?

LEXY: But he always insists so powerfully on the divorce of Socialism from Christianity. He will undo all the good we have been doing. Of course you know best; but—[*he shrugs his shoulders and wanders to the hearth beside Burgess*].

CANDIDA [*coaxingly*] Oh, do go, James. We'll all go.

BURGESS [*grumblingly*] Look ere, Candy! I say! Lets stay at home by the fire, comfortable. He wont need to be more'n a couple-o-hour away.

CANDIDA: Youll be just as comfortable at the meeting. We'll all sit on the platform and be great people.

MARCHBANKS [*terrified*] Oh please dont let us go on the platform. No: everyone will stare at us: I couldnt. I'll sit at the back of the room.

CANDIDA: Dont be afraid. Theyll be too busy looking at James to notice you.

MORELL: Prossy's complaint, Candida! Eh?

CANDIDA [*gaily*] Yes: Prossy's complaint.

BURGESS [*mystified*] Prossy's complaint! What are you talkin about, James?

MORELL [*not heeding him, rises; goes to the door; and holds it open, calling in a commanding tone*] Miss Garnett.

PROSERPINE [*in the distance*] Yes, Mr Morell. Coming.

They all wait, except Burgess, who turns stealthily to Lexy.

BURGESS: Listen ere, Mr Mill. Whats Prossy's complaint? Whats wrong with er?

LEXY [*confidentially*] Well, I dont exactly know; but she spoke very strangely to me this morning. I'm afraid she's a little out of her mind sometimes.

BURGESS [*overwhelmed*] Why, it must be catchin! Four in the same ouse!

PROSERPINE [*appearing on the threshold*] What is it, Mr Morell?

MORELL: Telegraph to the Guild of St Matthew that I am coming.

PROSERPINE [*surprised*] Dont they expect you?

MORELL [*peremptorily*] Do as I tell you.

    Proserpine, frightened, sits down at her typewriter, and obeys. Morell, now unaccountably resolute and forceful, goes across to Burgess. Candida watches his movements with growing wonder and misgiving.

MORELL: Burgess: you dont want to come.

BURGESS: Oh, dont put it like that, James. It's ony that it aint Sunday, you know.

MORELL: I'm sorry. I thought you might like to be introduced to the chairman. He's on the Works Committee of the County Council, and has some influence in the matter of contracts. [*Burgess wakes up at once*]. Youll come?

BURGESS [*with enthusiasm*] Cawrse I'll come, James. Aint it awlus a pleasure to ear you!

MORELL [*turning to Prossy*] I shall want you to take some notes at the meeting, Miss Garnett, if you have no other engagement. [*She nods, afraid to speak*]. You are coming, Lexy, I suppose?

LEXY: Certainly.

CANDIDA: We're all coming, James.

MORELL: No: you are not coming; and Eugene is not coming. You will stay here and entertain him—to celebrate your return home. [*Eugene rises, breathless*].

CANDIDA: But, James—

MORELL [*authoritatively*] I insist. You do not want to come; and he does not want to come. [*Candida is about to protest*]. Oh, dont concern yourselves: I shall have plenty of people without you: your chairs will be wanted by unconverted people who have never heard me before.

CANDIDA [*troubled*] Eugene: wouldnt you like to come?

MORELL: I should be afraid to let myself go before Eugene: he is so critical of sermons. [*Looking at him*] He knows I am afraid of him: he told me as much this morning. Well, I shall shew him how much afraid I am by leaving him here in your custody, Candida.

MARCHBANKS [*to himself, with vivid feeling*] Thats brave. Thats beautiful.

CANDIDA [*with anxious misgiving*] But—but—Is anything the matter, James? [*Greatly troubled*] I cant understand—

MORELL [*taking her tenderly in his arms and kissing her on the forehead*] Ah, I thought it was *I* who couldnt understand, dear.

ACT III

Past ten in the evening. The curtains are drawn, and the lamps lighted. The typewriter is in its case: the large table has been cleared and tidied: everything indicates that the day's work is over.

Candida and Marchbanks are sitting by the fire. The reading lamp is on the mantelshelf above Marchbanks, who is in the small chair, reading aloud. A little pile of manuscripts and a couple of volumes of poetry are on the carpet beside him. Candida is in the easy chair. The poker, a light brass one, is upright in her hand. Leaning back and looking intently at the point of it, with her feet stretched towards the blaze, she is in a waking dream, miles away from her surroundings and completely oblivious of Eugene.

MARCHBANKS [*breaking off in his recitation*] Every poet that ever lived has put that thought into a sonnet. He must: he cant help it. [*He looks to her for assent, and notices her absorption in the poker*]. Havnt you been listening? [*No response*]. Mrs Morell!

CANDIDA [*starting*] Eh?

MARCHBANKS: Havnt you been listening?

CANDIDA [*with a guilty excess of politeness*] Oh yes. It's very nice. Go on, Eugene. I'm longing to hear what happens to the angel.

MARCHBANKS [*letting the manuscript drop from his hand to the floor*] I beg your pardon for boring you.

CANDIDA: But you are not boring me, I assure you. Please go on. Do, Eugene.

MARCHBANKS: I finished the poem about the angel quarter of an hour ago. Ive read you several things since.

CANDIDA [*remorsefully*] I'm so sorry, Eugene. I think the poker must have hypnotized me. [*She puts it down*].

MARCHBANKS: It made me horribly uneasy.

CANDIDA: Why didnt you tell me? I'd have put it down at once.

MARCHBANKS: I was afraid of making you uneasy too. It looked as if it were a weapon. If I were a hero of old I should have laid my drawn sword between us. If Morell had come in he would have thought you had taken up the poker because there was no sword between us.

CANDIDA [*wondering*] What? [*With a puzzled glance at him*] I cant quite follow that. Those sonnets of yours have perfectly addled me. Why should there be a sword between us?

MARCHBANKS [*evasively*] Oh, never mind. [*He stoops to pick up the manuscript*].

CANDIDA: Put that down again, Eugene. There are limits to my appetite for poetry: even your poetry. Youve been reading to me for more than two hours, ever since James went out. I want to talk.

MARCHBANKS [*rising, scared*] No: I mustnt talk. [*He looks round him in his lost way, and adds, suddenly*] I think I'll go out and take a walk in the park. [*He makes for the door*].

CANDIDA: Nonsense: it's closed long ago. Come and sit down on the hearth-rug, and talk moonshine as you usually do. I want to be amused. Dont you want to?

MARCHBANKS [*half in terror, half enraptured*] Yes.

CANDIDA: Then come along. [*She moves her chair back a little to make room*].

He hesitates; then timidly stretches himself on the hearth-rug, face upwards, and throws back his head across her knees, looking up at her.

MARCHBANKS: Oh, Ive been so miserable all the evening, because I was doing right. Now I'm doing wrong; and I'm happy.

CANDIDA [*tenderly amused at him*] Yes: I'm sure you feel a great grown-up wicked deceiver. Quite proud of yourself, arnt you?

MARCHBANKS [*raising his head quickly and turning a little to look round at her*] Take care. I'm ever so much older than you, if you only knew. [*He turns quite over on his knees, with his hands clasped and his arms on her lap, and speaks with growing impulse, his blood beginning to stir*]. May I say some wicked things to you?

CANDIDA [*without the least fear or coldness, and with perfect respect for his passion, but with a touch of her wisehearted maternal humor*] No. But you may say anything you really and truly feel. Anything at all, no matter what it is. I am not afraid, so long as it is your real self that speaks, and not a mere attitude: a gallant attitude, or a wicked attitude, or even a poetic attitude. I put you on your honor and truth. Now say whatever you want to.

MARCHBANKS [*the eager expression vanishing utterly from his lips and nostrils as his eyes light up with pathetic spirituality*] Oh, now I cant say anything: all the words I know belong to some attitude or other—all except one.

CANDIDA: What one is that?

MARCHBANKS [*softly, losing himself in the music of the name*] Candida, Candida, Candida, Candida, Candida. I must say that now, because you have put me on my honor and truth; and I never think or feel Mrs Morell: it is always Candida.

CANDIDA: Of course. And what have you to say to Candida?

MARCHBANKS: Nothing but to repeat your name a thousand times. Dont you feel that every time is a prayer to you?

CANDIDA: Doesnt it make you happy to be able to pray?

MARCHBANKS: Yes, very happy.

CANDIDA: Well, that happiness is the answer to your prayer. Do you want anything more?

MARCHBANKS: No: I have come into Heaven, where want is unknown.

    Morell comes in. He halts on the threshold, and takes in the scene at a glance.

MORELL [*grave and self-contained*] I hope I dont disturb you.

    Candida starts up violently, but without the smallest embarrassment, laughing at herself. Eugene, capsized by her sudden movement, recovers himself without rising, and sits on the rug hugging his ankles, also quite unembarrassed.

CANDIDA: Oh, James, how you startled me! I was so taken up with Eugene that I didn't hear your latchkey. How did the meeting go off? Did you speak well?

MORELL: I have never spoken better in my life.

CANDIDA: That was first rate! How much was the collection?

MORELL: I forgot to ask.

CANDIDA [*to Eugene*] He must have spoken splendidly, or he would never have forgotten that. [*To Morell*] Where are all the others?

MORELL: They left long before I could get away: I thought I should never escape. I believe they are having supper somewhere.

CANDIDA [*in her domestic business tone*] Oh, in that case, Maria may go to bed. I'll tell her. [*She goes out to the kitchen*].

MORELL [*looking sternly down at Marchbanks*] Well?

MARCHBANKS [*squatting grotesquely on the hearth-rug, and actually at ease with Morell: even impishly humorous*] Well?

MORELL: Have you anything to tell me?

MARCHBANKS: Only that I have been making a fool of myself here in private whilst you have been making a fool of yourself in public.

MORELL: Hardly in the same way, I think.

MARCHBANKS [*eagerly, scrambling up*] The very, very, very same way. I have been playing the Good Man. Just like you. When you began your heroics about leaving me here with Candida—

MORELL [*involuntarily*] Candida!

MARCHBANKS: Oh yes: Ive got that far. But dont be afraid. Heroics are infectious: I caught the disease from you. I swore not to say a word in your absence that I would not have said a month ago in your presence.

MORELL: Did you keep your oath?

MARCHBANKS [*suddenly perching himself on the back of the easy chair*] It kept itself somehow until about ten minutes ago. Up to that moment I went on desperately reading to her—reading my own poems—anybody's poems—to stave off a conversation. I was standing outside the gate of Heaven, and refusing to go in. Oh, you cant think how heroic it was, and how uncomfortable! Then—

MORELL [*steadily controlling his suspense*] Then?

MARCHBANKS [*prosaically slipping down into a quite ordinary attitude on the seat of the chair*] Then she couldnt bear being read to any longer.

MORELL: And you approached the gate of Heaven at last?

MARCHBANKS: Yes.

MORELL: Well? [*Fiercely*] Speak, man: have you no feeling for me?

MARCHBANKS [*softly and musically*] Then she became an angel; and there was a flaming sword that turned every way, so that I couldnt go in; for I saw that that gate was really the gate of Hell.

MORELL [*triumphantly*] She repulsed you!

MARCHBANKS [*rising in wild scorn*] No, you fool: if she had done that I should never have seen that I was in Heaven already. Repulsed me! You think that would have saved us! virtuous indignation! Oh, you are not worthy to live in the same world with her. [*He turns away contemptuously to the other side of the room*].

MORELL [*who has watched him quietly without changing his place*] Do you think you make yourself more worthy by reviling me, Eugene?

MARCHBANKS: Here endeth the thousand and first lesson. Morell: I dont think much of your preaching after all: I believe I could do it better myself. The man I want to meet is the man that Candida married.

MORELL: The man that—? Do you mean me?

MARCHBANKS: I dont mean the Reverend James Mavor Morell, moralist and windbag. I mean the real man that the Reverend James must have hidden somewhere inside his black coat: the man that Candida loved. You cant make a woman like Candida love you by merely buttoning your collar at the back instead of in front.

MORELL [*boldly and steadily*] When Candida promised to marry me, I was the same moralist and windbag you now see. I wore my black coat; and my collar was buttoned behind instead of in front. Do you think she would have loved me any the better for being insincere in my profession?

MARCHBANKS [*on the sofa, hugging his ankles*] Oh, she forgave you, just as she forgives me for being a coward, and a weakling, and what you call a snivelling little whelp and all the rest of it. [*Dreamily*] A woman like that has divine insight: she loves our souls, and not our follies and vanities and illusions, nor our collars and coats, nor any other of the rags and tatters we are rolled up in. [*He reflects on this for an instant: then turns intently to question Morell*]. What I want to know is how you got past the flaming sword that stopped me.

MORELL: Perhaps because I was not interrupted at the end of ten minutes.

MARCHBANKS [*taken aback*] What!

MORELL: Man can climb to the highest summits; but he cannot dwell there long.

MARCHBANKS [*springing up*] It's false: there can he dwell for ever, and there only. It's in the other moments that he can find no rest, no sense of the silent glory of life. Where would you have me spend my moments, if not on the summits?

MORELL: In the scullery, slicing onions and filling lamps.

MARCHBANKS: Or in the pulpit, scrubbing cheap earthenware souls?

MORELL: Yes, that too. It was there that I earned my golden moment, and the right, in that moment, to ask her to love me. *I* did not take the moment on credit; nor did I use it to steal another man's happiness.

MARCHBANKS [*rather disgustedly, trotting back towards the fireplace*] I have no doubt you conducted the transaction as honestly as if you were buying a pound of cheese. [*He stops on the brink of the hearth-rug, and adds, thoughtfully, to himself, with his back turned to Morell*] I could only go to her as a beggar.

MORELL [*starting*] A beggar dying of cold! asking for her shawl!

MARCHBANKS [*turning, surprised*] Thank you for touching up my poetry. Yes, if you like: a beggar dying of cold, asking for her shawl.

MORELL [*excitedly*] And she refused. Shall I tell you why she refused? I can tell you, on her own authority. It was because of—

MARCHBANKS: She didnt refuse.

MORELL: Not!

MARCHBANKS: She offered me all I chose to ask for: her shawl, her wings, the wreath of stars on her head, the lilies in her hand, the crescent moon beneath her feet—

MORELL [*seizing him*] Out with the truth, man: my wife is my wife: I want no more of your poetic fripperies. I know well that if I have lost her love and you have gained it, no law will bind her.

MARCHBANKS [*quaintly, without fear or resistance*] Catch me by the shirt collar, Morell: she will arrange it for me afterwards as she did this morning. [*With quiet rapture*] I shall feel her hands touch me.

MORELL: You young imp, do you know how dangerous it is to say that to me? Or [*with a sudden misgiving*] has something made you brave?

MARCHBANKS: I'm not afraid now. I disliked you before: that was why I shrank from your touch. But I saw today—when she tortured you—that you love her. Since then I have been your friend: you may strangle me if you like.

MORELL [*releasing him*] Eugene: if that is not a heartless lie— if you have a spark of human feeling left in you—will you tell me what has happened during my absence?

MARCHBANKS: What happened! Why, the flaming sword [*Morell stamps with impatience*]—Well, in plain prose, I loved her so exquisitely that I wanted nothing more than the happiness of being in such love. And before I had time to come down from the highest summits, you came in.

MORELL [*suffering deeply*] So it is still unsettled. Still the misery of doubt.

MARCHBANKS: Misery! I am the happiest of men. I desire nothing now but her happiness. [*In a passion of sentiment*]

Oh, Morell, let us both give her up. Why should she have to choose between a wretched little nervous disease like me, and a pig-headed parson like you? Let us go on a pilgrimage, you to the east and I to the west, in search of a worthy lover for her: some beautiful archangel with purple wings—

MORELL: Some fiddlestick! Oh, if she is mad enough to leave me for you, who will protect her? who will help her? who will work for her? who will be a father to her children? [*He sits down distractedly on the sofa, with his elbows on his knees and his head propped on his clenched fists*].

MARCHBANKS [*snapping his fingers wildly*] She does not ask those silly questions. It is she who wants somebody to protect, to help, to work for: somebody to give her children to protect, to help and to work for. Some grown up man who has become as a little child again. Oh, you fool, you fool, you triple fool! I am the man, Morell: I am the man. [*He dances about excitedly, crying*] You dont understand what a woman is. Send for her, Morell: send for her and let her choose between— [*The door opens and Candida enters. He stops as if petrified*].

CANDIDA [*amazed, on the threshold*] What on earth are you at, Eugene?

MARCHBANKS [*oddly*] James and I are having a preaching match; and he is getting the worst of it.

Candida looks quickly round at Morell. Seeing that he is distressed, she hurries down to him, greatly vexed.

CANDIDA: You have been annoying him. Now I wont have it, Eugene: do you hear? [*She puts her hand on Morell's shoulder, and quite forgets her wifely tact in her anger*]. My boy shall not be worried: I will protect him.

MORELL [*rising proudly*] Protect!

CANDIDA [*not heeding him: to Eugene*] What have you been saying?

MARCHBANKS [*appalled*] Nothing. I—

CANDIDA: Eugene! Nothing?

MARCHBANKS [*piteously*] I mean—I—I'm very sorry. I wont do it again: indeed I wont. I'll let him alone.

MORELL [*indignantly, with an aggressive movement towards Eugene*] Let me alone! You young—

CANDIDA [*stopping him*] Sh!—no: let me deal with him, James.

MARCHBANKS: Oh, youre not angry with me, are you?

CANDIDA [*severely*] Yes I am: very angry. I have a good mind to pack you out of the house.

MORELL [*taken aback by Candida's vigor, and by no means relishing the position of being rescued by her from another man*] Gently, Candida, gently. I am able to take care of myself.

CANDIDA [*petting him*] Yes, dear: of course you are. But you musnt be annoyed and made miserable.

MARCHBANKS [*almost in tears, turning to the door*] I'll go.

CANDIDA: Oh, you neednt go: I cant turn you out at this time of night. [*Vehemently*] Shame on you! For shame!

MARCHBANKS [*desperately*] But what have I done?

CANDIDA: I know what you have done: as well as if I had been here all the time. Oh, it was unworthy! You are like a child: you cannot hold your tongue.

MARCHBANKS: I would die ten times over sooner than give you a moment's pain.

CANDIDA [*with infinite contempt for this puerility*] Much good your dying would do me!

MORELL: Candida, my dear: this altercation is hardly quite seemly. It is a matter between two men; and I am the right person to settle it.

CANDIDA: Two men! Do you call that a man! [*To Eugene*] You bad boy!

MARCHBANKS [*gathering a whimsically affectionate courage from the scolding*] If I am to be scolded like a boy, I must make a boy's excuse. He began it. And he's bigger than I am.

CANDIDA [*losing confidence a little as her concern for Morell's dignity takes the alarm*] That cant be true. [*To Morell*] You didnt begin it, James, did you?

MORELL [*contemptuously*] No.

MARCHBANKS [*indignant*] Oh!

MORELL [*to Eugene*] You began it: this morning. [*Candida, instantly connecting this with his mysterious allusion in the afternoon to something told him by Eugene in the morning, looks at him with quick suspicion. Morell proceeds, with the emphasis of offended superiority*] But your other point is true. I am certainly the bigger of the two, and, I hope, the stronger, Candida. So you had better leave the matter in my hands.

CANDIDA [*again soothing him*] Yes, dear; but—[*troubled*] I dont understand about this morning.

MORELL [*gently snubbing her*] You need not understand, my dear.

CANDIDA: But James, I [*the street bell rings*]—Oh bother! Here they all come. [*She goes out to let them in*].

MARCHBANKS [*running to Morell*] Oh, Morell, isnt it dreaful? She's angry with us: she hates me. What shall I do?

MORELL [*with quaint desperation, walking up and down the middle of the room*] Eugene: my head is spinning round. I shall begin to laugh presently.

MARCHBANKS [*following him anxiously*] No, no: she'll think Ive thrown you into hysterics. Dont laugh.

Boisterous voices and laughter are heard approaching. Lexy Mill, his eyes sparkling, and his bearing denoting unwonted elevation of spirit, enters with Burgess, who is greasy and self-complacent, but has all his wits about him. Miss Garnett, with her smartest hat and jacket on, follows them; but though her eyes are brighter than before, she is evidently a prey to misgiving. She places herself with her back to her typewriting table, with one hand on it to steady herself, passing the other across her forehead as if she were a little tired and giddy. Marchbanks relapses into shyness and edges away into the corner near the window, where Morell's books are.

LEXY [*exhilarated*] Morell: I must congratulate you. [*Grasping his hand*] What a noble, splendid, insipred address you gave us! You surpassed yourself.

BURGESS: So you did, James. It fair kep me awake to the lars' word. Didnt it, Miss Gornett?

PROSERPINE [*worriedly*] Oh, I wasnt minding you: I was trying to make notes. [*She takes out her notebook, and looks at her stenography, which nearly makes her cry*].

MORELL: Did I go too fast, Pross?

PROSERPINE: Much too fast. You know I cant do more than ninety words a minute. [*She relieves her feelings by throwing her notebook angrily beside her machine, ready for use next morning*].

MORELL [*soothingly*] Oh well, well, never mind, never mind, never mind. Have you all had supper?

LEXY: Mr Burgess has been kind enough to give us a really splendid supper at the Belgrave.

BURGESS [*with effusive magnanimity*] Dont mention it, Mr Mill. [*Modestly*] Youre arty welcome to my little treat.

PROSERPINE: We had champagne. I never tasted it before. I feel quite giddy.

MORELL [*surprised*] A champagne supper! That was very handsome. Was it my eloquence that produced all this extravagance?

LEXY [*rhetorically*] Your eloquence, and Mr Burgess's goodness of heart. [*With a fresh burst of exhilaration*] And what a very fine fellow the chairman is, Morell! He came to supper with us.

MORELL [*with long drawn significance, looking at Burgess*] O-o-o-h! the chairman. Now I understand.

Burgess covers with a deprecatory cough a lively satisfaction with his own diplomatic cunning. Lexy folds his arms and leans against the head of the sofa in a high-spirited attitude after nearly losing his balance. Candida comes in with glasses, lemons, and a jug of hot water on a tray.

CANDIDA: Who will have some lemonade? You know our rules: total abstinence. [*She puts the tray on the table, and takes up the lemon squeezer, looking enquiringly round at them*].

MORELL: No use, dear. Theyve all had champagne. Pross has broken her pledge.

CANDIDA [*to Proserpine*] You dont mean to say youve been drinking champagne!

PROSERPINE [*stubbornly*] Yes I do. I'm only a beer teetotaller, not a champagne teetotaller. I dont like beer. Are there any letters for me to answer, Mr Morell?

MORELL: No more tonight.

PROSERPINE: Very well. Goodnight, everybody.

LEXY [*gallantly*] Had I not better see you home, Miss Garnett?

PROSERPINE: No thank you. I shant trust myself with anybody tonight. I wish I hadnt taken any of that stuff. [*She takes un-*

certain aim at the door; dashes at it; and barely escapes without disaster].

BURGESS [*indignantly*] Stuff indeed! That gurl dunno what champagne is! Pommery and Greeno at twelve and six a bottle. She took two glasses amost straight horff.

MORELL [*anxious about her*] Go and look after her, Lexy.

LEXY [*alarmed*] But if she should really be— Suppose she began to sing in the street, or anything of that sort.

MORELL: Just so: she may. Thats why youd better see her safely home.

CANDIDA: Do, Lexy: theres a good fellow. [*She shakes his hand and pushes him gently to the door*].

LEXY: It's evidently my duty to go. I hope it may not be necessary. Goodnight, Mrs Morell. [*To the rest*] Goodnight. [*He goes. Candida shuts the door*].

BURGESS: He was gushin with hextra piety hisself arter two sips. People carnt drink like they huseter. [*Bustling across to the hearth*] Well, James: it's time to lock up. Mr Morchbanks: shall I ave the pleasure of your company for a bit o the way ome?

MARCHBANKS [*affrightedly*] Yes: I'd better go. [*He hurries towards the door; but Candida places herself before it, barring his way*].

CANDIDA [*with quiet authority*] You sit down. Youre not going yet.

MARCHBANKS [*quailing*] No: I—I didnt mean to. [*He sits down abjectly on the sofa*].

CANDIDA: Mr Marchbanks will stay the night with us, papa.

BURGESS: Oh well, I'll say goodnight. So long, James. [*He shakes hands with Morell, and goes over to Eugene*]. Make em give you a nightlight by your bed, Mr Morchbanks: itll comfort you if you wake up in the night with a touch of that complaint of yores. Goodnight.

MARCHBANKS: Thank you: I will. Goodnight, Mr. Burgess. [*They shake hands. Burgess goes to the door*].

CANDIDA [*intercepting Morell, who is following Burgess*] Stay here, dear: I'll put on papa's coat for him. [*She goes out with Burgess*].

MARCHBANKS [*rising and stealing over to Morell*] Morell: theres going to be a terrible scene. Arnt you afraid?

MORELL: Not in the least.

MARCHBANKS: I never envied you your courage before. [*He puts his hand appealingly on Morell's forearm*]. Stand by me, wont you?

MORELL [*casting him off resolutely*] Each for himself, Eugene. She must choose between us now.

    Candida returns. Eugene creeps back to the sofa like a guilty schoolboy.

CANDIDA [*between them, addressing Eugene*] Are you sorry?

MARCHBANKS [*earnestly*] Yes. Heartbroken.

CANDIDA: Well then, you are forgiven. Now go off to bed like a good little boy: I want to talk to James about you.

MARCHBANKS [*rising in great consternation*] Oh, I cant do that, Morell. I must be here. I'll not go away. Tell her.

CANDIDA [*her suspicions confirmed*] Tell me what? [*His eyes avoid hers furtively. She turns and mutely transfers the question to Morell*].

MORELL [*bracing himself for the catastrophe*] I have nothing to tell her, except [*here his voice deepens to a measured and mournful tenderness*] that she is my greatest treasure on earth—if she is really mine.

CANDIDA [*coldly, offended by his yielding to his orator's instinct and treating her as if she were the audience at the Guild of St Matthew*] I am sure Eugene can say no less, if that is all.

MARCHBANKS [*discouraged*] Morell: she's laughing at us.

MORELL [*with a quick touch of temper*] There is nothing to laugh at. Are you laughing at us, Candida?

CANDIDA [*with quiet anger*] Eugene is very quick-witted, James. I hope I am going to laugh; but I am not sure that I am not going to be very angry. [*She goes to the fireplace, and stands there leaning with her arm on the mantelpiece, and her foot on the fender, whilst Eugene steals to Morell and plucks him by the sleeve*].

MARCHBANKS [*whispering*] Stop, Morell. Dont let us say anything.

MORELL [*pushing Eugene away without deigning to look at him*] I hope you dont mean that as a threat, Candida.

CANDIDA [*with emphatic warning*] Take care, James. Eugene: I asked you to go. Are you going?

MORELL [*putting his foot down*] He shall not go. I wish him to remain.

MARCHBANKS: I'll go. I'll do whatever you want. [*He turns to the door*].

CANDIDA: Stop! [*He obeys*]. Didnt you hear James say he wished you to stay? James is master here. Dont you know that?

MARCHBANKS [*flushing with a young poet's rage against tyranny*] By what right is he master?

CANDIDA [*quietly*] Tell him, James.

MORELL [*taken aback*] My dear: I dont know of any right that makes me master. I assert no such right.

CANDIDA [*with infinite reproach*] You dont know! Oh, James! James! [*To Eugene, musingly*] I wonder do you understand, Eugene! [*He shakes his head helplessly, not daring to look at her*]. No: youre too young. Well, I give you leave to stay: to stay and learn. [*She comes away from the hearth and places herself between them*]. Now, James! whats the matter? Come: tell me.

MARCHBANKS [*whispering tremulously across to him*] Dont.

CANDIDA: Come. Out with it!

MORELL [*slowly*] I meant to prepare your mind carefully, Candida, so as to prevent misunderstanding.

CANDIDA: Yes, dear: I am sure you did. But never mind: I shant misunderstand.

MORELL: Well—er— [*he hesitates, unable to find the long explanation which he supposed to be available*].

CANDIDA: Well?

MORELL [*blurting it out badly*] Eugene declares that you are in love with him.

MARCHBANKS [*frantically*] No, no, no, no, never. I did not, Mrs Morell: it's not true. I said I loved you. I said I understood you, and that he couldnt. And it was not after what passed there before the fire that I spoke: it was not, on my word. It was this morning.

CANDIDA [*enlightened*] This morning!

MARCHBANKS: Yes. [*He looks at her, pleading for credence, and then adds simply*] That was what was the matter with my collar.

CANDIDA: Your collar? [*Suddenly taking in his meaning she turns to Morell, shocked*]. Oh, James: did you—[*she stops*]?

MORELL [*ashamed*] You know, Candida, that I have a temper to struggle with. And he said [*shuddering*] that you despised me in your heart.

CANDIDA [*turning quickly to Eugene*] Did you say that?

MARCHBANKS [*terrified*] No.

CANDIDA [*almost fiercely*] Then James has just told me a falsehood. Is that what you mean?

MARCHBANKS: No, no: I—I—[*desperately*] it was David's wife. And it wasn't at home: it was when she saw him dancing before all the people.

MORELL [*taking the cue with a debater's adroitness*] Dancing before all the people, Candida; and thinking he was moving their hearts by his mission when they were only suffering from—Prossy's complaint. [*She is about to protest: he raises his hand to silence her*]. Don't try to look indignant, Candida—

CANDIDA: Try!

MORELL [*continuing*] Eugene was right. As you told me a few hours after, he is always right. He said nothing that you did not say far better yourself. He is the poet, who sees everything; and I am the poor parson, who understands nothing.

CANDIDA [*remorsefully*] Do you mind what is said by a foolish boy, because I said something like it in jest?

MORELL: That foolish boy can speak with the inspiration of a child and the cunning of a serpent. He has claimed that you belong to him and not to me; and, rightly or wrongly, I have come to fear that it may be true. I will not go about tortured with doubts and suspicions. I will not live with you and keep a secret from you. I will not suffer the intolerable degrada-

tion of jealousy. We have agreed—he and I—that you shall
choose between us now. I await your decision.

CANDIDA [*slowly recoiling a step, her heart hardened by his
rhetoric in spite of the sincere feeling behind it*] Oh! I am to
choose am I? I suppose it is quite settled that I must belong
to one or the other.

MORELL [*firmly*] Quite. You must choose definitely.

MARCHBANKS [*anxiously*] Morell: you dont understand. She
means that she belongs to herself.

CANDIDA [*turning to him*] I mean that, and a good deal more,
Master Eugene, as you will both find out presently. And
pray, my lords and masters, what have you to offer for my
choice? I am up for auction, it seems. What do you bid,
James?

MORELL [*reproachfully*] Cand— [*He breaks down: his eyes
and throat fill with tears: the orator becomes a wounded an-
imal*]. I cant speak—

CANDIDA [*impulsively going to him*] Ah, dearest—

MARCHBANKS [*in wild alarm*] Stop: it's not fair. You musnt
shew her that you suffer, Morell. I am on the rack too; but I
am not crying.

MORELL [*rallying all his forces*] Yes: you are right. It is not for
pity that I am bidding. [*He disengages himself from Candida*].

CANDIDA [*retreating, chilled*] I beg your pardon, James: I did
not mean to touch you. I am waiting to hear your bid.

MORELL [*with proud humility*] I have nothing to offer you but
my strength for your defence, my honesty for your surety, my
ability and industry for your livelihood, and my authority
and position for your dignity. That is all it becomes a man to
offer to a woman.

CANDIDA [*quite quietly*] And you, Eugene? What do you offer?

MARCHBANKS: My weakness. My desolation. My heart's need.

CANDIDA [*impressed*] Thats a good bid, Eugene. Now I know
how to make my choice.

*She pauses and looks curiously from one to the other, as if
weighing them. Morell, whose lofty confidence has changed
into heart-breaking dread at Eugene's bid, loses all power of*

concealing his anxiety. Eugene, strung to the highest tension, does not move a muscle.

MORELL [in a suffocated voice: the appeal bursting from the depths of his anguish] Candida!

MARCHBANKS [aside, in a flash of contempt] Coward!

CANDIDA [significantly] I give myself to the weaker of the two. Eugene divines her meaning at once: his face whitens like steel in a furnace.

MORELL [bowing his head with the calm of collapse] I accept your sentence, Candida.

CANDIDA: Do you understand, Eugene?

MARCHBANKS: Oh, I feel I'm lost. He cannot bear the burden.

MORELL [incredulously, raising his head and voice with comic abruptness] Do you mean me, Candida?

CANDIDA [smiling a little] Let us sit and talk comfortably over it like three friends. [To Morell] Sit down, dear. [Morell, quite lost, takes the chair from the fireside: the children's chair]. Bring me that chair, Eugene. [She indicates the easy chair. He fetches it silently, even with something like cold strength, and places it next Morell, a little behind him. She sits down. He takes the visitor's chair himself, and sits, inscrutable. When they are all settled she begins, throwing a spell of quietness on them by her calm, sane, tender tone]. You remember what you told me about yourself, Eugene: how nobody has cared for you since your old nurse died: how those clever fashionable sisters and successful brothers of yours were your mother's and father's pets: how miserable you were at Eton: how your father is trying to starve you into returning to Oxford: how you have had to live without comfort or welcome or refuge: always lonely, and nearly always disliked and misunderstood, poor boy!

MARCHBANKS [faithful to the nobility of his lot] I had my books. I had Nature. And at last I met you.

CANDIDA: Never mind that just at present. Now I want you to look at this other boy here! my boy! spoiled from his cradle. We go once a fortnight to see his parents. You should come with us, Eugene, to see the pictures of the hero of that household. James as a baby! the most wonderful of all babies. James holding his first school prize, won at the ripe age of eight! James as the captain of his eleven! James in his first frock coat! James under all sorts of glorious circumstances! You know how strong he is (I hope he didnt hurt you): how clever he is: how happy. [*With deepening gravity*] Ask James's mother and his three sisters what it cost to save James the trouble of doing anything but be strong and clever and happy. Ask me what it costs to be James's mother and three sisters and wife and mother to his children all in one. Ask Prossy and Maria how troublesome the house is even when we have no visitors to help us to slice the onions. Ask the tradesmen who want to worry James and spoil his beautiful sermons who it is that puts them off. When there is money to give, he gives it: when there is money to refuse, I refuse it. I build a castle of comfort and indulgence and love for him, and stand sentinel always to keep little vulgar cares out. I make him master here, though he does not know it, and could not tell you a moment ago how it came to be so. [*With sweet irony*] And when he thought I might go away with you, his only anxiety was—what should become of me! And to tempt me to stay he offered me [*leaning forward to stroke his hair caressingly at each phrase*] his strength for my defence! his industry for my livelihood! his dignity for my position! his—[*relenting*] ah, I am mixing up your beautiful cadences and spoiling them, am I not, darling? [*She lays her cheek fondly against his*].

MORELL [*quite overcome, kneeling beside her chair and embracing her with boyish ingenuousness*] It's all true, every word. What I am you have made me with the labor of your hands and the love of your heart. You are my wife, my mother, my sisters: you are the sum of all loving care to me.

CANDIDA [*in his arms, smiling, to Eugene*] Am I your mother and sisters to you, Eugene?

MARCHBANKS [*rising with a fierce gesture of disgust*] Ah, never. Out, then, into the night with me!

CANDIDA [*rising quickly*] You are not going like that, Eugene?

MARCHBANKS [*with the ring of a man's voice—no longer a*

boy's—in the words] I know the hour when it strikes. I am impatient to do what must be done.

MORELL [*who has also risen*] Candida: dont let him do anything rash.

CANDIDA [*confident, smiling at Eugene*] Oh, there is no fear. He has learnt to live without happiness.

MARCHBANKS: I no longer desire happiness: life is nobler than that. Parson James: I give you my happiness with both hands: I love you because you have filled the heart of the woman I loved. Goodbye. [*He goes towards the door*].

CANDIDA: One last word. [*He stops, but without turning to her. She goes to him*]. How old are you, Eugene?

MARCHBANKS: As old as the world now. This morning I was eighteen.

CANDIDA: Eighteen! Will you, for my sake, make a little poem out of the two sentences I am going to say to you? And will you promise to repeat it to yourself whenever you think of me?

MARCHBANKS [*without moving*] Say the sentences.

CANDIDA: When I am thirty, she will be forty-five. When I am sixty, she will be seventy-five.

MARCHBANKS [*turning to her*] In a hundred years, we shall be the same age. But I have a better secret than that in my heart. Let me go now. The night outside grows impatient.

CANDIDA: Goodbye. [*She takes his face in her hands; and as he divines her intention and falls on his knees, she kisses his forehead. Then he flies out into the night. She turns to Morell, holding out her arms to him*]. Ah, James!

They embrace. But they do not know the secret in the poet's heart.

Composition and Cast List

Composition begun 2 October 1894; completed 7 December 1894. Published in *Plays Pleasant and Unpleasant*, 1898. Revised text in Collected Edition, 1930. Copyright reading at the Theatre Royal, South Shields, on 30 March 1895. First presented by the Independent Theatre Company at Her Majesty's Theatre, Aberdeen, on 30 July 1897, at the start of a provincial tour. Presented by the Stage Society at the Strand Theatre, London, on 1 July 1900, with the same cast except for the substitution of Granville Barker as Eugene Marchbanks (originally spelled Marjoribanks).

THE REVEREND JAMES MAVOR MORELL
Charles Charrington
EUGENE MARCHBANKS   *Courtney Thorpe*
MR BURGESS   *Lionel Belmore*
THE REVEREND ALEXANDER MILL   *Robert Farquharson*
MISS PROSERPINE GARNETT   *Edith Craig*
CANDIDA MORELL   *Janet Achurch*

Scene: The Study and General Sitting-room, St Dominic's Vicarage, Victoria Park, London. Time: October 1894.

ACT I   *Morning*
ACT II   *Afternoon*
ACT III   *Evening*

Appendix

In 1904, Shaw wrote his short play *How He Lied to Her Husband*, a title that alludes to the code of honor of courtly poetry also of concern in *Candida*, which burlesqued the themes of *Candida* and replicated its dramatic situation to show that its Candida muse-figure, Aurora Bompas, is unmistakably philistine. The holograph manuscript of the short play has a digression cut from the published version that makes clear the link between *Candida* and *Parsifal*. Shaw wrote *How He Lied* for Arnold Daly, the original Eugene in America, as a curtain raiser to his first short play, *The Man of Destiny,* written just after *Candida*:

She—What did you get tickets for?—Parsifal?

He—I tried; but Parsifal was sold out for tonight. (*He takes out two Vaudeville Theatre tickets*).

She—Then what did you get?

He—Can you ask me? What is there besides Parsifal that we two could endure, except Candida?

She—(*springing up*) Candida! No, I wont go to it again, Henry. . . . It is that play that has done all the mischief. I'm very sorry I ever saw it: it ought to be stopped.

He—(*amazed*) Aurora!

She—Yes: I mean it.

He—That divinest love poem—the poem that gave us courage to speak to one another—that revealed to us what we really felt for one another—that—

She—Just so. It put a lot of stuff into my head that I should never have dreamt of for myself. I imagined myself just like Candida.

He—(*catching her hands and looking earnestly at her*) You
were right. You *are* like Candida.

She—(*snatching her hands away*) Oh, stuff! And I thought
you were just like Eugene. (*Looking critically at him*) Now
that I come to look at you, you *are* rather like him, too.
(*Applause and laughter. Mr. Arnold Daly grins feebly
at the audience*).
—Play Resumed—

From *Candida & How He Lied to Her Husband: Facsimiles of
the Holograph Manuscripts*, introduction by J. Percy Smith
(New York: Garland, 1981, 204–206).

The Bernard Shaw Library featuring the definitive texts prepared
under the editorial supervision of Dan H. Laurence

Arms and the Man
Introduction by Rodelle Weintraub
Raina, a young Bulgarian woman with romantic notions of war and an idealized
view of her soldier fiancé, is surprised one night by a Swiss mercenary soldier
seeking refuge in her bedchamber. The pragmatic Captain Bluntschli proceeds, in
the course of one of Shaw's most delightful comedies, to puncture all of Raina's
illusions about love, heroism, and class. Optimistic, farcical, absurd, and teeming
with sexual energy, *Arms and the Man* has Shaw inverting the devices of melodra-
ma to glorious effect.   *ISBN 0-14-303976-8*

Caesar and Cleopatra
Introduction by Stanley Weintraub
In a cheeky nod to Shakespeare's towering reputation, Shaw reinvents two of his
historical characters but sets his own play in a period predating both *Julius Caesar*
and *Antony and Cleopatra*. Shaw's Cleopatra is kittenish girl with a streak of cruelty, while his Caesar is a world-weary philosopher-soldier who is as much a
stranger in Rome as in the barbaric court of Egypt. With wit and irony, *Caesar
and Cleopatra* satirizes Shakespeare's use of history and comments wryly on the
politics of Shaw's own time. With its undertone of melancholy, it is one of his
most affecting plays.   *ISBN 0-14-303977-6*

Candida
Introduction by Peter Gahan
The Reverend Morell, a Socialist preacher, brings a young penniless poet, Eugene
Marchbanks, into his home, which is dominated by his fascinating wife, Candida.
With its single stage setting and small cast of six characters, this play of Shaw's is
deceptively simple. Centered on a romantic triangle and parodying courtly love
and the domestic drama of Ibsen, *Candida* also abounds with classical allusions,
the fervor of a religious revival, and poetic inspiration and aspirations.
                                                           ISBN 0-14-303978-4

Heartbreak House
Introduction by David Hare
Set during a house party at the eccentric household of Captain Shotover and his
daughter Hesione, this comedy of manners takes a probing look at the conflict
between "old-fashioned" idealism and the realities of the modern age. *Heartbreak
House* was Shaw's own favorite play.   *ISBN 0-14-043787-8*

Major Barbara
Introduction by Margery Moran
In this sparkling comedy, Andrew Undershaft is a millionaire armaments dealer
obsessed with money and hostile toward the poor. His energetic daughter
Barbara, however, is a devout major in the Salvation Army. She sees her father as
just another soul to be saved. But when the Salvation Army needs funds to keep
going, it is Undershaft who saves the day.   *ISBN 0-14-043790-8*

Man and Superman
Introduction by Stanley Weintraub
John Tanner, author of *The Revolutionist's Handbook*, is horrified to discover that Ann Whitefield intends to marry him and flees, with the young woman in hot pursuit, on a chase that eventually leads to the underworld. A wonderfully original twist on the Don Juan myth, this finely tuned combination of intellectual seriousness and popular comedy is a classic exposé of the eternal struggle between the sexes.
ISBN 0-14-043788-6

Pygmalion
Introduction by Nicholas Grene
Shaw radically reworks Ovid's tale to give it a feminist slant: While Henry Higgins successfully teaches Eliza to speak and act like a duchess, she asserts her independence, adamantly refusing to be his creation. A brilliantly witty exposure of the British class system, the exceedingly entertaining *Pygmalion* remains one of Shaw's most popular plays.
ISBN 0-14-143950-5

Saint Joan
Introduction by Joley Wood
"On Playing Joan" by Imogen Stubbs
With *Saint Joan*, Shaw reached the height of his fame as a dramatist. Fascinated by the story of Joan of Arc (canonized in 1920), but unhappy with "the whitewash which disfigures her beyond recognition," he presents a realistic Joan: proud, intolerant, naive, foolhardy, always brave—a rebel who challenged the conventions and values of her day.
ISBN 0-14-043791-6

Plays Pleasant
Introduction by W. J. McCormack
Plays Pleasant comprises four comedies intended not only to amuse audiences but also to provoke them. *Arms and the Man*, set in the Balkan mountains, satirizes romantic views of war and military heroism. *Candida* presents the complicated relationship between a vicar, his wife, and her young admirer. *The Man of Destiny* is a witty war of words between a "strange lady" and a Napoleon Bonaparte at odds with English mores. The exuberant farce *You Never Can Tell* presents an aging suffragette and a divided family reunited by chance.   ISBN 0-14-043794-0

Plays Unpleasant
Introduction by David Edgar
With *Plays Unpleasant*, Shaw broke all the rules governing how a playwright should entertain his audience. In *Widowers' Houses*, Harry Trench's engagement to Blanche Sartorius is called into question when he realizes that her father is a slum landlord. In *The Philanderer*, charismatic Leonard Charteris proposes marriage to Grace while still involved with the beautiful Julia Craven—but Julia is not inclined to surrender him so easily. And in *Mrs. Warren's Profession*, Vivie must reconsider her own life when she discovers that her mother's immoral earnings have paid for her genteel upbringing.
ISBN 0-14-043793-2

Three Plays for Puritans
Introduction by Michael Billington
Disgusted and bored by the trend for titillation and sham on the London stage, Shaw wrote these plays both to educate and to entertain his audiences. In *The Devil's Disciple*, a clergyman turned soldier—the Shavian ideal of a Puritan hero—willingly risks his life for a stranger. The brilliant historical satire *Caesar and Cleopatra* contains unexpected portraits of its title characters. In *Captain Brassbound's Conversion*, it is Lady Cicely's cunning manipulation of the truth that ensures that fairness, rather than justice, prevails.
ISBN 0-14-043792-4

CLICK ON A CLASSIC
www.penguinclassics.com

The world's greatest literature at your fingertips

Constantly updated information on more than a thousand titles,
from Icelandic sagas to ancient Indian epics, Russian drama to
Italian romance, American greats to African masterpieces

•

The latest news on recent additions to the list, updated
editions, and specially commissioned translations

•

Original essays by leading writers

•

A wealth of background material, including biographies
of every classic author from Aristotle to Zamyatin, plot
synopses, readers' and teachers' guides, useful web links

•

Online desk and examination copy assistance for academics

•

Trivia quizzes, competitions, giveaways, news on
forthcoming screen adaptations

FOR THE BEST IN PAPERBACKS, LOOK FOR THE

In every corner of the world, on every subject under the sun, Penguin represents quality and variety—the very best in publishing today.

For complete information about books available from Penguin—including Penguin Classics, Penguin Compass, and Puffins—and how to order them, write to us at the appropriate address below. Please note that for copyright reasons the selection of books varies from country to country.

In the United States: Please write to *Penguin Group (USA), P.O. Box 12289 Dept. B, Newark, New Jersey 07101-5289* or call 1-800-788-6262.

In the United Kingdom: Please write to *Dept. EP, Penguin Books Ltd, Bath Road, Harmondsworth, West Drayton, Middlesex UB7 0DA.*

In Canada: Please write to *Penguin Books Canada Ltd, 90 Eglinton Avenue East, Suite 700, Toronto, Ontario M4P 2Y3.*

In Australia: Please write to *Penguin Books Australia Ltd, P.O. Box 257, Ringwood, Victoria 3134.*

In New Zealand: Please write to *Penguin Books (NZ) Ltd, Private Bag 102902, North Shore Mail Centre, Auckland 10.*

In India: Please write to *Penguin Books India Pvt Ltd, 11 Panchsheel Shopping Centre, Panchsheel Park, New Delhi 110 017.*

In the Netherlands: Please write to *Penguin Books Netherlands bv, Postbus 3507, NL-1001 AH Amsterdam.*

In Germany: Please write to *Penguin Books Deutschland GmbH, Metzlerstrasse 26, 60594 Frankfurt am Main.*

In Spain: Please write to *Penguin Books S. A., Bravo Murillo 19, 1° B, 28015 Madrid.*

In Italy: Please write to *Penguin Italia s.r.l., Via Benedetto Croce 2, 20094 Corsico, Milano.*

In France: Please write to *Penguin France, Le Carré Wilson, 62 rue Benjamin Baillaud, 31500 Toulouse.*

In Japan: Please write to *Penguin Books Japan Ltd, Kaneko Building, 2-3-25 Koraku, Bunkyo-Ku, Tokyo 112.*

In South Africa: Please write to *Penguin Books South Africa (Pty) Ltd, Private Bag X14, Parkview, 2122 Johannesburg.*

Printed in the United States
by Baker & Taylor Publisher Services